The Disaster Recovery Handbook
&
Household Inventory Guide

What Others Are Saying About This Book

"Since 1992, I have used *The Household Inventory Guide* as a bible to assist clients to help settle insurance claims and to calculate IRS casualty loss deductions due to losses from fires, floods, and other disasters. I have also used the book extensively with clients to find out if they are properly insured. Most assume they are until I show them the household contents lists and ask them again. Adding the insurance and tax chapters in the book is a real coup!"
Robert L. Castle, CPA, Oakland, California

"An early version of the material in this book was a significant factor in the successful insurance negotiations of many of the families in the 1993 and 2003 wildfires in Southern California. This easy-to-follow guide will make it easier to recall what you owned and will help facilitate discussion with your insurance company. It also is a valuable tool for setting up your new household."
Ursula Hyman, Esq., Chair, Eaton Canyon Recovery Alliance

"Amy Bach and Carol Ingalls Custodio have combined their talents and backgrounds to provide a comprehensive, easy to read resource. This organized and informative book covers everything that any disaster survivor would need to know. Even though I am in the disaster preparedness business, I found the book refreshingly informative and helpful. This handbook cannot prevent bad things from coming our way, but it can help minimize the negative impact that a disaster can have on our life and the lives of those we love. As a Fire Chief, I have access to countless publications on disaster preparedness. Amy and Carol's handbook is the one I will have in my home and the one that I will rely upon most for the protection of my own home and family."
Phil Kleinheinz, Fire Chief, City of Santa Clara, CA

"Custodio and Bach have packed this indispensable handbook with some of the most practical, valuable guidance any survivor of a catastrophic loss could ever hope to have. Insurers may not like all of what's in it, but that should be the best news any survivor should want to hear. But why wait for a loss? Put your hands on a copy of this handbook and read it for the wisdom and ideas it contains. Then attach it to your homeowner's insurance policy and store the two items together in your safe deposit box. Ideally, you'll never need to read either again. But if you do, you can trust that two smart and savvy women and their friends are watching your back."
Paul Vandeventer, President & CEO, and Community Partners Coordinator, 2003 California Fire Recovery Initiative

The Disaster Recovery Handbook
&
Household Inventory Guide

*How to Recount and Recover from
Your Losses after a Fire, Flood, Earthquake,
Hurricane, or Tornado*

Amy Bach
Carol Ingalls Custodio

with contributions by
Karen Reimus
Susan I. Knowles

united policyholders

San Francisco

A Note from the Authors

This book has been written to provide information about the subject matter covered. It is sold with the understanding that the authors and publisher are not engaged in rendering legal, accounting, or other professional services or advice. If legal or other expert assistance is required, the services of a competent professional should be sought.

It is not the purpose of the book to reprint all the possible information that may otherwise be available to the public, but rather to offer a starting point on the road to recovery after a substantial property loss. You are urged to read all available information, whether from private publishers, nonprofits, or government organizations

Every effort has been made to make this book complete and accurate. However, there may be mistakes both typographical and in content. Although the personal property inventories here are very extensive, they cannot be 100% comprehensive. The authors and publisher have neither liability nor responsibility to any person or entity with respect to any loss or damage caused, or alleged to be caused, directly or indirectly, by this book or by the information contained herein.

Cover photo by Steve Cole.

Printed in the United States of America

For more information, contact:
(510) 763-9740 or email info@unitedpolicyholders.org
For permission to use material from this book, submit a written request to:
United Policyholders, PMB 262, 110 Pacific Ave., San Francisco, CA 94111

ISBN: 0-9785043-0-5

Library of Congress Control Number: 2006902651

Dedication

*For those who have suffered the loss of a home
and the many individuals and groups
who helped them start over.*

Contents

Introduction   *ix*

About the Authors   *x*
   Karen Reimus, Chapter 1
   Amy Bach, Chapters 2–5
   Susan Knowles, Chapter 6
   Carol Ingalls Custodio, Chapters 7–34

The Inside Story   *xiv*

Acknowledgments   *xvii*

1   Steps on the Road to Recovery: What Disaster Survivors Need to Know   *1*

2   Insurance Recovery 101: Basic Tips to Collect What You're Owed   *15*

3   How to Inventory and Get Paid Fairly for Your Damaged or Destroyed Personal Property / Contents Items   *35*

4   Dwelling Tips: How to Get a Fair Settlement on Your Damaged or Destroyed Home   *43*

5   Frequently Asked Questions about Insurance Issues   *49*

6   Tax Help for Casualty and Disaster Victims   *56*

7   Making Lists & Making Sense of These Lists   *73*

8   The Short List   *75*

9   Appliances, Furniture, & Furnishings   *81*

10   Electronics/Technology   *86*

11   Kitchen   *89*

12   Dining Room   *98*

13 Living and/or Family Room *100*

14 Bedroom *102*

15 Bathroom *106*

16 The Laundry Area (Including Cleaning Equipment & Supplies) *109*

17 Office & School Supplies *111*

18 Outdoor Living *114*

19 Storage Spaces — Small & Large *117*

20 Emergency Supplies *121*

21 Infants & Toddlers *125*

22 Kids' Stuff *128*

23 Pet Supplies *130*

24 Recreation, Sports, & Exercise *132*

25 Travel *136*

26 Camping & Backpacking *138*

27 Books (Fiction & Nonfiction) *141*

28 Music Categories *144*

29 Movie Genres *146*

30 Art, Hobbies, & Collections *147*

31 The Car *151*

32 Records, Documents, & The Safe Deposit Box *153*

33 Shopping Green *156*

34 Preparing for Emergencies: Learning from Experience *159*

Index *164*

Introduction

Losing one's home as a result of a catastrophic event is a devastating experience. Recovery is generally a long and difficult process that presents practical, emotional, and financial challenges. There is no need for disaster survivors to re-invent the wheel as they begin the process. The tips in this book from previous disaster survivors and recovery aid experts provide invaluable help overcoming the common challenges.

The Disaster Recovery Handbook & Household Inventory Guide is a collaborative effort by experts who either lost a home in a disaster or who have experience helping others who have suffered such a loss. This guide lays out practical steps for survivors to take on the road to recovery. It contains comprehensive lists of household items and detailed information about anticipating and avoiding insurance obstacles, as well as tax help—specifically for disaster recovery.

This updated book has roots in its predecessor, *The Household Inventory Guide*, which was written in the aftermath of the 1991 Oakland-Berkeley firestorm as an aid to the residents of some 3,000 homes that were reduced to ashes in an historic urban area wildfire. Since its first publication, 6,500 copies of what is sometimes referred to as "the little yellow book" have made their way around the United States, following fires, floods, earthquakes, hurricanes, and tornadoes. People across the country have used the lists to help compile the copious household contents inventories required by their insurance companies and/or the IRS and to help them replace lost items.

This expanded guide contains updated and improved versions of the detailed lists that were so popular in the original book, plus the added benefit of tips for overcoming the full range of challenges that survivors routinely face. Our goal is to help survivors take a "big picture" look at the road ahead—the road that others have navigated before them—and to help them move forward with sure footing every step of the way.

About the Authors

Contributor **Karen Reimus** (Chapter 1) is a lawyer and married mother of two. Karen and her family lost their home and all their possessions in the October 1993 Cedar Fire. The firestorm, the largest wildfire in California state history, leveled her suburban San Diego neighborhood.

Finding herself underinsured by a top-rated insurance company despite having a brand new policy, Karen not only fought for her own rights with her insurer, she also felt compelled to fight to protect other homeowners facing the same insurance nightmares she had encountered after losing her home. She became actively involved in the fight for legislative reform in the area of homeowner's insurance. Reimus was one of twelve Southern California Wildfire survivors labeled "The Dynamic Dozen" by State Insurance Commissioner John Garamendi, who personally lobbied state legislators to pass reformative homeowner's insurance legislation.

She remains involved in grassroots lobbying efforts to support homeowner's insurance reform, and is active in her local Fire Safe Council promoting fire safety by proper brush clearance and weed abatement in areas on or near the California wildland-urban interface.

In addition to contributing to this book and doing advocacy work for insurance reform, Karen and her neighbors formed a fire recovery group called "The Burnout Sisters" to provide mutual emotional support and to facilitate the exchange of information. The group continued meeting after rebuilds were completed, and to mark the second anniversary of the firestorm, the Burnout Sisters organized a house tour of rebuilt homes and raised $16,000 for the American Red Cross.

Amy Bach (Chapters 2–5), one of the preeminent insurance consumer advocates in the United States, began her career in 1983 as an insurance analyst with the New York Consumer Protection Board, an executive branch state agency. An attorney, Bach currently serves as the Executive Director of United Policyholders (UP), a nationally recognized not-for-profit organization that is dedicated to educating the public on insurance issues and consumer rights.

Bach has worked closely with untold numbers of individuals and business owners, insurance company personnel, local, statewide and national public officials and recovery aid workers in regions throughout California, Arizona, New Mexico, Texas, Florida, Oregon, Mississippi, and Louisiana following large-scale natural disasters.

During her 20-year career Bach has helped draft legislation, regulations, and consumer publications on virtually every type of insurance product. She has conducted consumer surveys and engaged in countless debates and initiatives relating to insurance public policy. Bach relocated from New York to California in the late 80s, where she earned a law degree while working part time on projects related to insurance.

Bach has performed government service on insurance matters for the California Attorney General's Office, as a consultant to the California State Senate, and as counsel to a special master overseeing court-ordered reforms at the California Department of Insurance. She has successfully tried cases against insurance companies as an attorney representing individual and commercial insureds. She has experience relating to pricing and sales issues as well as the nuts and bolts of property, auto, and disability claim adjusting.

To establish a source of reliable information and support for insurance policyholders after the 1989 Loma Prieta earthquake, Amy and colleague Ina DeLong co-founded UP in 1991 (www.uphelp.org). Bach has served on the board since its inception and is now UP's primary spokesperson.

Amy lives in San Francisco with her husband and two children.

Contributor **Susan I. Knowles**, B.S., M.A., (Chapter 6) is an enrolled agent, licensed to practice before the Internal Revenue Service. In August 1994 the "Highway 41 Fire" in San Luis Obispo County, California shot flames down a canyon like a Bunsen burner tipped on its side. The burn was fierce and incredibly fast moving. Susan, her husband, and their two teenagers lost their home and everything in it.

The Knowles had evaluated their insurance coverage in January of that year, so their coverage was quite adequate. Although their insurance company provided very satisfactory service following their loss, they still needed help learning how to "speak the language" of claims—residential, personal property, and temporary living. Fortunately, United Policyholders arrived to serve as a resource, helping the survivors through a very difficult process. Subsequently, when the fires swept through Southern California in the fall of 2003, Susan contacted United Policyholders to find out how she could help her southern neighbors. She became the Web site moderator for UP's Fire Bulletin Board, responding to questions regarding tax impact.

In addition to other work projects, for more than nine years Susan has owned and operated Knowles-Enrolled Agent, a financial and management consulting firm engaged in income tax return preparation, estate and gift tax return preparation, investment analysis, financial analysis, and business equity appraisals.

Knowles is the author of several articles, including articles published in *Pacific Coast Business Magazine*: "What Your Tax Return Tells Your Banker" and "Determining the Value of Your Business." She also wrote "When You Give It Away, It Is Gone...Or Is It?" published in the *California Enrolled Agent* magazine. Susan's Web site is www.knowlesoffice.com.

Carol Ingalls Custodio, M.S. in Counseling (Chapters 7–34) was living and working as a career counselor in the San Francisco Bay Area when the Oakland–Berkeley firestorm destroyed over 3,000 dwellings in October 1991.  Knowing many of the fire survivors personally and aware of their losses, she wrote and self-published *The Household Inventory Guide: Ideas and Lists for Stocking, Restocking, and Taking Stock of Your Home.* Then Carol Phillips, she later married Clark Custodio, a deputy fire chief she met at a disaster conference.

During the 1990s, Custodio became interested in emergency preparedness and disaster recovery and was invited to participate as a vendor at earthquake preparedness and safety fairs. She published 6,500 copies of "the little yellow book," that managed to make its way into the hands of disaster survivors all over the country. Carol and her husband now live in Ashland, Oregon, where they are part of a local neighborhood CERT (Community Emergency Response Team). They have three adult sons.

The Inside Story

The making of this book is a story in itself. The theme "paying it forward," comes from a book by Catherine Ryan Hyde in which a 12-year-old boy takes on an extra-credit Social Studies assignment to "Think of an idea for world change, and put it into action." His idea was to do a good deed for three people, and, in exchange, ask each of them to "pay it forward" to three more. The good deeds would grow exponentially.

In *our* story, the first good deeds happened after the 1991 fire in the Northern California Oakland-Berkeley hills that destroyed more than 3,000 homes. The devastated community gradually became organized and educated through meetings sponsored by a newly formed not-for-profit called United Policyholders (UP). UP's core message is that mutual support and information sharing are the best path to disaster recovery. The North Hills Phoenix Association, a civic group, also formed and partnered with UP. Connections were being made and people were reaching out to one another.

Bay Area resident **Carol Custodio** (then Carol Phillips) did not lose her home but was inspired to help those who did by writing and self-publishing this book's predecessor, *The Household Inventory Guide.* The *Guide* was a "lifesaver" for disaster survivors struggling with the onerous task of recreating an inventory of a life's worth of possessions. Because it was a valuable complement to UP's educational materials, the organization publicized the book throughout the United States.

Two years later, some 400 homes were destroyed in a 1993 wildfire in the Laguna Beach area of Southern California. UP sent emissaries, and another "phoenix" association rose from the ashes called Laguna Relief. Northern readers of Carol's book paid her good deed forward by reaching out to their counterparts in the south. Carol's friend, **Sari Kulberg**, called a friend in Laguna to see if she was okay. Although her home had been spared, many of her friends were not so fortunate, so Sari shared her copy of *The Household Inventory Guide*. That friend showed it to some of her friends, and word spread. As a result, two nonprofit groups pooled their resources and bought enough copies of Carol's book to give one to every family who had lost a home in the fire.

One of the recipients of the "little yellow book" was Laguna Beach resident **Fred Sharman** and his wife, Ceil. The Sharmans used the lists in the book to help them detail their losses for their insurance company. Ten years later, when Fred was serving as the Director of Lauguna Relief, he arranged to buy the remainder of Carol's books and donated them to three separate communities in need. Fred urged Carol to republish her book and was an important contributor to this new version.

Word continued to spread about Carol's book as one community recovering from disaster lent support to the next. **Ursula Hyman** had used it in her work with a post-wildfire civic group called the Eaton Canyon Recovery Alliance that was helping neighbors recover from a devastating 1995 wildfire.

When a far-ranging fire in 2003 destroyed more than 3,000 structures in Southern California, Ursula reached out again, and received permission from Carol to make copies of her out-of-print *Guide* so no one in need would be deprived of access to its helpful content.

After **Lila Hayes'** mother's home was destroyed by those same 2003 fires, she became the Director of an "Old Fire Recovery Group" that helped residents of San Bernadino County recover. Lila's group members used Carol's book, and Lila made suggestions to the authors that became part of this updated and expanded version.

UP Executive Director and co-founder **Amy Bach** approached Carol Custodio (Chapters 7–34) in 2005 to form a working group to republish her book. Amy (Chapters 2–5) brought enthusiasm, insurance expertise, and a wide network of contacts to the project, including contributing authors **Karen Reimus** and **Susan Knowles**.

Karen (Chapter 1) lived in one of three communities that received copies of Carol's book from Fred Sharman's organization, Laguna Relief, in 2003. She had treasured it as a resource that helped her recover from the total destruction of her home.

Susan Knowles (Chapter 6) knows personally and professionally how critical it is to access financial advice from prior disaster survivors. Her small community was destroyed by a wildfire, and because the financial obstacles to recovering from the loss of one's home are so formidable and time-consuming, she knows firsthand how "paying it forward" has a particular value when it comes to sound tax advice.

Something amazing about the human spirit wants to lend a helping hand to people in distress. It happens to individuals and to groups. So many people who have been touched personally by one disaster or another continue to be involved in disaster recovery efforts, emergency preparedness efforts, or both. We are, after all, one big village.

Acknowledgments

The *Disaster Recovery Handbook and Household Inventory Guide* is a collaborative effort by the writers and a wide circle of professional and personal associates. We extend hearty and heartfelt thanks to the following people for their significant contributions:

We thank **Bob Castle**, an Oakland, California CPA who participated in brainstorming sessions and shared his expertise in post-disaster tax issues and enthusiasm for the republication project. Laguna Beach, California community leader and disaster survivor **Fred Sharman** contributed many wise suggestions and served as a long distance cheerleader, applauding our efforts along the way.

Production coordinator **Mary Douglas**, Rogue Valley Publications, skillfully shepherded us through the publication process and assembled a team that included copyeditor **Ruth Cottrell**, who did a masterful job of making sure our words made sense and were sensibly placed, and graphic designer **David Ruppe**, Impact Publications, who not only designed the book's contents and cover, but also did all of the typesetting.

We thank and acknowledge **Kelly Prichett** and the members, donors and Board of Directors of United Policyholders. Last but not least, we thank our devoted spouses, **Clark Custodio** and **Jeff Fox** for their support, feedback and assistance.

Chapter 1

Steps on the Road to Recovery

What Disaster Survivors Need to Know

How do you begin the recovery process when everything you own is gone? The key word here is *process,* and you begin it slowly, one step at a time. The purpose of this book is to ease your journey on the road to recovery by sharing insights, tips, and lessons learned by others who have had the problems you are facing now.

Our home and all my family's possessions burned to the ground in one of the large wildfires that California periodically experiences. We were out of town when the fire hit, and we literally lost everything we owned. We were not allowed into the neighborhood for two days, as fire crews worked to put out all remaining "hot spots." When we arrived at the debris site that had once been our home, it was difficult to grasp the enormity of the loss. Could the ash we were stepping in really be all that was left? Sadly, the answer was yes. Following are some of the things learned that hopefully will help you in your recovery.

You may be reading this book because you recently experienced your own disaster. Feelings of grief, helplessness, and confusion, together with irrational behavior, are likely to be present in the wake of a major disaster. However, you may have already come to realize that you are not alone. You are on the road to

1

recovery, and help is at hand. All of us involved in writing this book hope to help guide you through the recovery process.

This book is intended to be as practical as possible. What you will find are all-encompassing lists of things to do or to avoid, along with an occasional reality check and tips regarding priorities. So sit quietly, scan through the pages for an overview, and then dive in. Keep this book by your side in the days and weeks ahead as you navigate the road to recovery.

Stepping into the Action Mode

Following a disaster, a number of things need to be addressed or taken care of as soon as possible. In order to get things accomplished, make a list of things to do each day. The number of things to do will seem endless. And, frankly, your mind may not be working as clearly as usual. You are likely to find that your mind will jump from problem to problem. Similarly, you are probably going to be tired, emotional, and stressed. To get through the coming weeks, it is critical that you prioritize things to be done and create a realistic list of items that can be accomplished each day.

Even if you have never been a list-maker, use this strategy to stay focused on the very large number of things that have to be handled. Each night make a list of things you need to accomplish the next day. Making this list may also have the added benefit of helping you sleep better. Knowing that you have already planned out the next day will help your mind "shut down" for the night.

A typical daily list may look something like this: Talk to children's teachers. Go to rental furniture store. Meet with insurance adjuster. Pick up groceries. Spend quality time with children. Return calls. Review insurance paperwork/policy.

If you or your family members are on medication, a number one item for your first list should be to **contact your pharmacist to get replacements for prescriptions or other medications.**

Try to deal with every item on your daily list. If that proves to be too much, reschedule items, including time for relaxation. Be sure to take some period of time each day to stop all activity and treat yourself to a long hot bath, read a short story, or share a cup of coffee with a friend. You will need breaks.

Action: Your First Steps

Take care of yourself and your family. Do whatever you need to do to take care of yourself physically to get through this incredibly stressful period. Do your best to get as much sleep as possible, and eat well because the recovery process is truly a marathon. If you are too wound up to sleep, consider calling your family physician and asking for a gentle sedative. This is not the time to "tough it out."

Insurance. If you have homeowner's or renter's insurance, call your insurance carrier and get the ball rolling to process your claim. Get an adjuster assigned to your claim as soon as possible so that you can begin receiving the benefits of your policy, such as money for temporary housing and clothing. Your adjuster may be able to provide a cash advance against your future claim. If an advance is not offered, ask for one!

If your insurance policy was destroyed, request a copy of it. **Read it.** You may find it very difficult to read and to understand, but it is critical that you try to grasp the rights and remedies afforded you under your policy. It is virtually impossible to effectively negotiate with your claims adjuster if you do not have a basic understanding of your rights under the policy. The following chapters on insurance will help you understand policy language and your rights. Also, keep in mind that after most large loss disasters, local bar associations offer free or low-cost attorney services to help you determine your rights. Make use of these services to educate yourself.

Temporary housing. If your loss occurred in a widespread natural disaster, **act as fast as possible to find a new place to live** because rental housing is going to go fast. If you wait to find a new place to live, you may end up living much further from your original home than you had planned. If you have children, that means that they (and you) may be commuting some distance each day to keep them in their original schools. (If your loss occurred in a single home-loss scenario, this piece of advice is less pressing). See the next chapter regarding Additional Living Expenses (ALE) consideration because you need an early education here.

Telecommunications. If you have a cellular telephone that you are using more than usual because your landline was destroyed, call your cell phone service provider to boost the number of minutes on your calling plan. Otherwise, following your disaster, you will probably be hit with an enormous cell phone bill. Also, frequently check your "minutes used" function to avoid running into extra minutes, which are usually charged at a very high rate.

Action: High Priority Matters

Be alert to immediate sources of financial assistance. If your loss has occurred in a large-scale disaster, nonprofit and other private organizations can provide immediate financial help. Groups like the Salvation Army and the Red Cross provide assistance. If a disaster recovery or FEMA center has been set up in your community, go there and explore all resources available to you. Be sure to return to the disaster assistance center(s) often. The number of groups offering assistance can increase daily. In the days following a disaster, city government, civic and religious groups, utility firms, and county and state offices may set up tables. All of these groups provide useful resources. For instance, at the cable television table the representatives may be able to waive the charges for your home's cable boxes that were destroyed. At the department of insurance table there may be valuable information about how to begin looking for reputable contractors. Local religious organizations may provide some cash, clothing, utensils or bedding to families affected, with no strings attached. So, stay attuned to offers of help that may spring up in your community.

Remember that these organizations are fixed on helping you NOW. But one day you will return, and these resources will have disappeared. You will be "yesterday's news." So take advantage of what they have to offer **now**.

Connect and disconnect services to your home. Some services like cable or the Internet do not charge based on usage, but rather a flat fee. Thus, you may end up paying for services you did not receive because your house was destroyed. Whom do you notify? The following companies need to be contacted to connect services to your new temporary living quarters while discontinuing services to your damaged or destroyed home.

- Telephone: For local and long distance services (landlines/cell phones) and to install phone jacks, if needed

- Heating/air Conditioning (i.e., gas, electric, propane, fuel oil, coal)
- Water
- Garbage
- Television (cable or satellite)
- Newspapers
- Water delivery

Don't be shy about asking for charges to be waived or reduced for lost items or equipment. For example, prior to the disaster, perhaps you had bottled water delivered. Obviously, all of the bottles would have been lost. Explain to your supplier how their bottles were destroyed, and the company may agree to waive any charges.

Action: Getting Organized

Lists: Keep a running list of personal property items that need to be replaced. Once you begin settling into temporary living quarters, there will be countless items that you will need to get. Keep a running list in a convenient place, either with you or near you, in order to eliminate unnecessary trips to stores or the donation centers. Since there will be so much happening in your life at this time, writing down needed replacement items is a must. Use the **Short List** chapter in this book to help you determine your immediate needs. Keep all your receipts to help you with your insurance company's personal property claim. You should also use a separate credit card for purchasing replacement items (See the **Tax Help** chapter for more details).

Accepting help from others. With seemingly interminable "to do" lists, be open to accepting help from others. This may be a new concept for someone who has been living independently. When you have suffered a catastrophic loss, people want to help. Let them! Even if you are the type of person who does not accept help easily, you need as much help as you can get. You are going to learn first-hand that it is a greater blessing to give than to receive. So, give your friends, family and yes, even strangers, a blessing—let them help you.

There are many ways people can help. For example, ask friends to be collection points for donation items for you and your family. Sorting through the items that become available for "free," either through direct donations or at collection centers, may be an overwhelming task. It can be incredibly time-consuming to rummage through the bags and piles of used clothing to determine which items your family can use. And, frankly, it's stressful. This is true especially if you have not ever been on the receiving end of charitable donations. You might consider asking a close friend to be your family's "personal shopper" to sort through donated items to find what you can and will use. This may be a huge help to you, and friends will be happy to able to do something useful to assist you.

Since you are coping with a catastrophic loss and relocating to a new living space at the same time, enlist friends to help with this also. Ask for help moving and settling into your temporary living quarters. Be specific about your needs. For example, ask for help to organize any donated items or to clean any salvaged items. Get help to organize kitchen and bathroom cabinets and drawers. Friends can organize bedroom drawers, shelves, and closets. They can label boxes for storage in the garage or call to set up services, such as telephone, cable, electricity, and water at your new place. There is much to do, and "many hands make light work."

Prioritize who needs to be informed. One task that can be assigned to helpers is to inform others of your change of address. Whom do you need to notify? Not all of the people and places suggested in this list need to be reached immediately. Set your priorities and keep notes as you check off these contacts.

- Friends and close friends out of the area
- Employers
- Schools
- Physicians
- Dentists
- Veterinarians
- Insurance companies
- Banks and financial or lending institutions
- Brokerage and/or investment firms
- Credit card companies or stores whose cards you hold
- Internal Revenue Service

- State Franchise Board
- Department of Motor Vehicles
- Appliance service contractors
- Business and professional groups
- Charitable organizations
- Church, synagogue, etc.
- Alumni associations or former schools
- Political parties
- Public and/or special interest groups
- Fraternal organizations
- Social groups or clubs
- Frequent flier programs
- Other membership groups
- Magazines, subscriptions, and catalogs

As you notify organizations of your address change, be sure to request replacement identification, membership cards, and other documents for those that you lost. Examples include driver's licenses, birth certificates, Social Security cards, passports, and estate documents. Also, remember to re-register to vote, either in person or by mail. You can pick up mail-in registration cards at your local city or town hall, public library, motor vehicle office, or social service agency. Magazines, subscriptions and catalogs will be helpful later in developing and pricing your insurance's personal property claim.

Helping your children cope. There are many things you can do to assist children in coping with the loss. For instance, try finding immediate replacements for emotional and comfort items. This is easier to do with younger children. If your children had favorite stuffed animals or toys, try to replace them with identical items, if possible. Younger children will often not comprehend that this is a "different" item and can be comforted by having something familiar or, at least, similar again.

Contact friends, family and teachers. If possible, keep your children in touch with people who comfort them. If they have favorite teachers at school, call the principal and ask to have the teachers call your children, wherever you're living, to say hello.

If practical, keep your children in the same schools as before the loss. This may mean commuting to their old schools, depending on the location of the temporary living quarters, but it will give the children some degree of stability and familiarity.

Explore counseling options for your children through their schools. Depending on the school district and the size of the loss, special counseling may be available through the schools to assist your children in coping with the loss. Also, the Red Cross provides help with mental health counselors.

Let your children talk as much as they want to about the loss event.

Action: Networking

Network as much as you can. If you are a private type of person, this is a good time to open up. Talk with other loss survivors if your loss has occurred in a catastrophic loss scenario. Talk with others about their insurance claim experiences. When you see neighbors and friends in the same situation, be sure to get their contact information so you can stay in touch with them. Other loss survivors are an invaluable source of information. They may be able to tell you how each insurance company is handling losses, provide you with sources of financial and other assistance that may be available, suggest good coping strategies, and so on.

If your loss occurred in an area-wide disaster, be sure to attend meetings held in your community regarding the loss. Do as much as you can to educate yourself regarding your policy and the claims process. It is very possible that there will be group meetings to discuss the topic of insurance. Set up, or be a part of, a network with others insured by the same insurance company. In a large disaster, insurance companies' adjusters discuss among themselves how the process is going and how claims are progressing. You also should network with others to close any information gap at your end.

Action: Your Household Inventory

Take control. The purpose of this book is to get you focused on the tasks ahead, to provide an organized path out of your disorganized world, to prepare you to work with your insurance company, and, specifically, to help you with one of the most daunting tasks you will face—completing your personal property inventory.

Complete your personal property inventory. The task of completing your personal property inventory is all about lists. This task is time-consuming and may be filled with sadness or anger. Completing the personal property inventory is one of the most, if not *the most*, overwhelming tasks in recovery from a total loss. But this task is also about recovering the dollars you have rightfully coming to you. You have paid for this peace of mind over the years. Now, you must take on a proactive role to claim what is your due.

What is personal property? An initial challenge may be trying to determine what is personal property versus what is not. An insurance adjuster once described it this way, "If you could take the roof off of your house, lift the house off the foundation and then turn the house over and shake it, whatever falls out of the house is personal property." That is a fairly accurate visualization.

What will be required to complete your personal property inventory? Your insurance company will probably require you to list items of personal property in your home so you can recover the money due you under the personal property coverage in your insurance policy. The amount of detail required in your personal property inventory will vary by insurance company. Some insurance companies can be fairly liberal in allowing you to group categories of items together on your inventory, and other insurance companies may want you to list every single item. Some may ask you to list the cost of the item at time of purchase, the age of the item lost, as well as its current replacement cost.

Getting started with your personal property inventory. Where do you start? Perhaps you will begin with nothing more than a yellow lined pad for each room in the house and lots of sharp pencils. In this initial stage, tap into your memory of the specific contents of each room—one room at a time. What were the big-ticket items or items unique to your family that were there the day of the disaster? This may include artwork, collections, cameras, silverware, and so on.

Revisit the rooms. Several days later, "revisit" or visualize the rooms again. Close your eyes and visualize walking into each room. For instance, start at one end of a room. What was on the walls and on the floor? Try to remember everything on a top bookshelf or cupboard shelf, and then work your way down to the bottom shelf, listing everything that you can recall on your inventory. Work your way around the room. Again, in your mind, open closets, cupboards, cabinets, and drawers to try to visualize what you kept in those places. Write those items on your inventory. It is a good idea to revisit each room more than once, and every family member should do this. You may have forgotten something that another family member will remember.

▶ **Do not concern yourself with adding dollar amounts at this time. Now is the time to mentally reconstruct your personal inventory.**

The forgotten stuff. As you start to complete the inventory of your rooms, you will to feel that you are forgetting "stuff." That "stuff" has value. If you saw a $5.00 bill on the ground, would you lean over and pick it up? What about a $20.00 bill? Every item you forget is potentially that $5.00 or $20.00 bill. Each item you forget is your money, and you will be leaving it on the table in your negotiations with your insurance company. How do you get those hard-to- remember items onto your yellow pads?

Lists. A big part of the solution lies in the lists in this book. After you have exhausted your memory, turn to the **Household Inventory Guide** chapters of this book. But remember that if you go there too early in the process, you will short circuit your memory of the unique items that you had that are not likely be found in these generic lists. The lists in this book contain items people typically have in their homes. These lists will help you to fill in the blanks, and they will help you to submit your complete inventory so that you don't leave your dollars on the table.

Allocate time. Completing the inventory is very time consuming. It can seem a truly overwhelming task at the outset. Try to set realistic goals to get it done. For example, set aside time to work on the inventory every day. Set a goal of completing a certain number of pages per day or per week. Your particular need to receive personal property funds from the insurance company may dictate how much time you should allocate for this task.

Friends and neighbors. Have friends and family look over your inventory to see if they can spot anything you missed. Friends and family have probably been to your home many times and may remember items that you have forgotten. Ask if they have any pictures of the inside of your home, taken while at parties or other get-togethers at your house. These can be especially helpful because you can scan them for details.

If your loss has occurred in a large-loss disaster, you may consider comparing your list with your neighbors' lists. Did they include something on their inventory lists that you also owned but forgot to put on yours?

Other sources for lists. Be careful about lists provided by your insurance company. All insurance companies offer basic lists. Lists available from insurance companies are limited, and if you start with these, your thought process will probably lead you to "forget" many items for the reasons we mentioned earlier. When you are ready for help with outside lists to fill in your inventory, you will find the lists in this book to be far more comprehensive than the ones from insurance companies.

You may find other lists also, but at this time your next task is assigning value to the items you have lost and moving forward in your recovery.

Assigning costs. Don't worry about attaching replacement valuations to the items initially; just try to get the items listed on the inventory to begin with. But when it is time to determine costs, you have some options. All your receipts were probably destroyed, so what can you do?

You should be able to find prices for many items by locating costs on the Internet. Virtually all national retail and discount stores have their own Web sites. Web sites such as Shopzilla.com and Gifts.com can help you comparison shop by showing a range of prices for the same product. Many of these same stores also have catalogs or "Sunday circulars" you can use.

Many stores now offer gift registry services that allow you to create a very helpful list by walking around the store with a scanner. Scan the items that you had before the loss. Then print out a copy of the registry, which will have not only the item listed on it but a current replacement value as well. You can use this same idea in other types of stores such as hardware, sporting goods, or grocery stores. You will need to speak to a manager and explain your situation. If they cooperate, you can gain valuable information and save time.

Remembering where you shopped originally can be important. Revisit those stores and sites. If you were not a discount shopper before the disaster, the pricing process is not a time to start. Do not list items at sale prices! The sales will probably be over by the time you go to replace your items.

Replacement costs vs. actual cash value (ACV). Replacement costs and ACV are discussed in the following chapters. You should be aware, however, that you may be required to state the age of items. Also understand that all items do not age at the same rate. This concept is also be explained. For now, simply determine the costs of purchasing your replacement items.

The emotional component: Seek emotional support from friends and family as you complete your inventory. Working on your inventory can be very emotionally trying. As a loss survivor, you may spend a lot of time trying to forget everything you lost, not remembering it. It is difficult to have to recall all the items that are now gone. In particular, emotionally charged items like a wedding dress, a child's toy, or the family picture albums can be difficult to recall without sadness. Have a friend or spouse work on the inventory with you if possible. A friend can provide much-needed emotional support and can shorten the time needed to complete the task. The inventory does go faster with two or more people helping.

Help is available for a cost. If you are unable to do your inventory, you may request that a personal property claims adjuster assist you. Many insurance companies can provide a personal property claims adjuster to help you complete your inventory. However, be warned that this route will probably leave a large portion of your claim unrecovered because an industry adjustor's purpose and your goal are not likely to be the same. Also, you may choose to hire a public adjustor. If you do, you will share the settlement you receive. This option is explored in the following chapters.

The final inventory report. The final completed inventory may be either handwritten or computer-generated, depending on your insurance company's requirements. There are computerized spreadsheet forms in EXCEL, or you can create your own. The latter option may be more appropriate for you if you are comfortable with computers. Whether you complete your household inventory by hand or on the computer, your insurance company will probably provide you with forms to be used in listing your items. Ask them if the lists that you are developing will be acceptable. If they want your lists on their forms, you can ask them to do it for you. But if they do so, check their work carefully for omissions or errors.

Some final thoughts about your personal property claim. First, from the practical side: The money you recover from your contents loss may be needed in another area that you don't want to contemplate. Building costs go up. Labor, supplies, and inflation will all become factors in the construction of your replacement home. Also, you may be underinsured. It is not uncommon that some of the dollars recovered in the contents portion of your claim will be needed to help you rebuild your house. So it is imperative that you spend the needed time to present a complete inventory.

Second, a look at the emotional side: Reviewing the extraordinary number of items on your completed form, you will probably discover that many of your things can't be replaced. It is important to remember that when a loss occurs, that loss generates grief, and grief is not just about people and relationships. It can also be about places and things and lifestyles. Our homes and what we keep in them say a lot about ourselves. They become part of our identity, especially as the years pile up along side the things we accumulate. When we lose our things, we feel as if a piece of ourselves is missing, and we can lose our balance. Because there were meanings and memories attached to those things, you will miss them and grieve. Please know that **this is normal**.

To understand your own responses to the catastrophic incident you experienced, keep in mind the classic five stages of grief that you can expect to pass through at one time or another. You may move through some stages quickly, others not so quickly, and you may even swing back and forth between the stages. The first stage is **denial** ("Oh no, not me"; "not my house"; "not my collectibles"). Then comes **anger** ("Who is responsible?"; "Why me?"; "Why can't I get the help I need?"). Later comes **bargaining**, typically addressed to a higher power ("If you will restore my house completely, I will donate to . . ."). **Depression** follows

(This will often be manifested by crying or inability to function). Finally, the last stage is **acceptance** ("It was only stuff; now let's move on with the recovery").

Much can be learned from a disaster that destroys your home. One of the most important lessons is that time heals. There is no doubt that you will always be saddened over some of the irreplaceable things you lost in the disaster. But give yourself a lot of time to come to terms with the losses you have suffered. As you pass through the various stages of grief, know that is okay to be sad and angry. With time come healing and acceptance.

Knowledge Is Power

Take control. Now that you have an overview of the days ahead, it is important for you to understand how you will be "made whole" again. This will happen by your gaining insight into the process, by your actions that follow this knowledge, by taking small steps daily, by help from friends, neighbors, and people you never knew and, ultimately, by your insurance company.

The next four chapters take you into a world most people never enter. You are about to travel deep into the world of homeowners insurance. Your policy is full of words that may be strange to you, legal talk, and numbers. You have been paying for protection over the years. Now it is time to learn how to collect the promised benefits.

Chapter 2

Insurance Recovery 101

Basic Tips to Help You Collect
What You're Owed

If your home has been damaged or destroyed and you have insurance, you probably have a steep learning curve ahead of you in order to collect what you're owed. You need to learn some basic facts about insurance claims. The basic facts presented in this chapter apply, regardless of the event that caused the loss or the type of company that insured you.

As you begin to pick up the pieces on your road to recovery, you need to understand that insurance is a vehicle to get you back home. But while you are thinking of your insurance policy as a car to drive you where you need to go, remember—it's not going to drive itself. You need to drive it. You paid for it. You've got the most at stake in making sure it gets you where you need to go. So now is the time to get a basic understanding of how your insurance policy is supposed to work for you, what problems you may encounter during the claim process, and what resources there are for getting help when you need it. Of course, insurance policies aren't really cars—they're contracts, and confusing ones at that. Let's get started.

What Do You Need to Know First?

First the good news. You're not alone. Help is available. You will get through the recovery process. Some insurers and adjusters treat their customers better than others by paying what they owe reasonably promptly. If you get up to speed on the basics of filing and getting paid on a large insurance claim, you will significantly increase your odds of getting a fair and prompt settlement.

Now some not so good news. Large and total loss claims usually take more than a full year to get fully and fairly paid. Pace yourself. This is a marathon, not a sprint. Some insurers and adjusters try to rush folks into fast settlements and close claims quickly without paying in full. There will be *a lot of misinformation* floating around about what's covered and what's not and how much it should cost to repair the damage.

And here's our news. It doesn't matter where you live—Washington, Louisiana, Mississippi, Florida, California, or Texas—the insurance claim process is the same.

When it comes to collecting on your insurance policy to replace the contents of your home or to restore it, it's all about **documentation, organization, and negotiation.** To get paid fully and reasonably promptly for your insurance claims, you need to **report a claim even if you think or have been told it may not be covered.** It's your property and your possessions. You paid for coverage and good claim service. If you're not getting it, be prepared to stand up for yourself.

When you deal with an insurance company on a claim where large dollar amounts are at stake, it's a business transaction. Insurance companies are profit-oriented businesses—not charities or "good neighbors." Don't confuse the ads they use to sell their products with reality. Your insurance adjuster may be friendly, but he or she is not your friend. If your losses were due to a natural disaster, make sure you work closely with other property owners who were struck by the same disaster and are dealing with their insurance companies. Keep in touch and trade information. Knowledge leads to money.

Get help when you need it. If you're overwhelmed by the process and need professional help, get it. Most people know nothing about insurance other than the ads they've seen, the premium bills they've paid, and perhaps a "fender bender" or plumbing leak claim that got settled with no problems.

If your property was severely damaged and you've paid for insurance protection, get smart! Because insurers are in the business of making money, that doesn't mean that they're evil or to be feared. It just means that you cannot sit back and trust them to take care of you if you want a fair shake. You need to do the work of documenting what you lost and how much it's *really* going to cost to replace it (all of it). Stand up for what you're entitled to, and get help when you need it.

Most disaster survivors end up knowing more about insurance than they ever wanted to know, and they'll tell you—knowledge leads to money. The more you know about the insurance claim process and your rights and your options for getting help, the more your insurer is going to pay.

The advice about insurance in this book has made it possible for many property owners to get on the road to recovery over the past 14 years. It comes from the work of a not-for-profit national organization called United Policyholders (UP). The organization is made up of professionals and volunteers with many years of personal experience, expertise, and first-hand knowledge about the business of insurance and large loss claims. For tips and advice on buying the right insurance and related topics, visit their website at **www.uphelp.org**. UP welcomes new members, questions, and e-mail at **info@unitedpolicyholders.org**.

The insurance information in this book is covered in four sections. Start by reading the **Basic Tips** below. The **Contents/ Personal Property** chapter will help you settle the part of your claim that covers replacement of the contents of your home. The **Dwelling Tips** chapter will help you settle the part of your claim that covers the repairs or reconstruction of your home. The fifth chapter responds to **Frequently Asked Questions.**

Basic Tips

▶ **Report your claim promptly, and read your policy.**

Get and read a complete and current copy of your policy from your insurance company as soon as possible. Locate complete and up-to-date copies of all policies on your home, property, and vehicles. If you're having trouble getting a complete copy of your policies, contact the government agency in your state that oversees insurance companies. Every state has one.

The page that states your name and address, policy number, dollar amounts of coverage, and "endorsement" codes is called your "**declarations page**" (called a Dec page). The policy will be hard to read and understand, but knowing what you're covered for is a critical first step in the claim process. Only you can protect your rights.

The main categories of coverage are: Dwelling, Other Structures (sometimes called "Additional" or "Appurtenant" Structures), Contents, and Additional Living Expenses, (sometimes called "Loss of Use"). Dwelling coverage is generally called "Coverage A." Contents coverage is generally called "Coverage C." Most policies contain an automatic increase to account for inflation and other categories of items that are covered via "endorsements" (additions to the basic policy).

Check the dollar amounts/limits for your main coverage categories. You'll need to do some math to figure out what your policy limits actually are. Don't rely solely on your insurer's or adjuster's calculations.

Read the "Endorsements" (extras) that apply to your policy. To find which endorsements you bought, check the Dec page and look for names or codes for policy extras. A typical endorsement is one that provides **Building Code or Ordinance** coverage. It gives you coverage for costs you'll incur from having to comply with local building codes. You need this because most policies exclude "betterment," meaning that they pay to replace only what you had. If building codes, laws, or ordinances require you to make improvements to get permit approval, this endorsement fills the gap in the coverage created by the exclusion in your basic policy.

Another common endorsement that gives you extra coverage is an "extended replacement cost" provision. If you bought this provision and your damage exceeds the dwelling limit stated on your Dec page, the extended replacement cost endorsement will kick in to give you more coverage. These endorsements generally give you an extra percentage in the range of 20% to 75% of your Dec page limit. Again, if you have such an endorsement, make sure you do your own math to calculate the percentage increase and figure out the total benefits you're owed. Find out if the percentage increase feature applies to raise the amount for other categories of coverage, such as Contents or Other Structures.

Basic contents limits are generally set by the insurance company as a percentage of your dwelling coverage limits. The standard contents limit is 75% of your dwelling coverage limits.

Check your limits for "scheduled" personal property items (i.e., artwork, jewelry, musical instruments, collections). Make sure that the policy limits and coverages are what you think you bought, what you asked for, and what you were promised by the agent and insurer that sold you the policy. If you are confused, **do not rely solely on your insurance company or adjuster for answers.** Visit UP's website and consult with someone who specializes in advising or representing insurance consumers (reputable public adjusters, attorneys who specialize in insurance matters, or contractors who have experience negotiating with insurance adjusters).

Underinsurance alert. Most property owners who suffer a large or total loss find that they don't have enough insurance coverage in at least one category. This is so common that there is a word to describe it: **underinsurance.** Dwelling coverage to pay for repairs or rebuilding is the most common category in which property owners are *underinsured.* If you are underinsured, get educated on your options. Look at United Policyholders' **Claim** section for tips on underinsurance at **www.uphelp.org.**

▶ **Notify your agent and insurance company promptly that your home is damaged or destroyed and that you are filing a claim.**

Even if you have been told your damage is not covered or may not exceed your deductible, you should notify your insurance company in writing that your property is destroyed or damaged and that you are filing a claim that you expect them to pay. There are economic reasons why agents, adjusters, and insurance company personnel sometimes discourage people from filing valid claims. There are also simple reasons. Insurance policies are written in confusing legalese. Even professionals often read them incorrectly.

▶ **Get a three-ring binder and get organized.**

The better you document your losses and stay organized in dealing with your insurance claim, the smoother the process will go. Set up a binder with a section for your **Dwelling Loss,** a section for your **Contents Loss**, and a section for your **Temporary Living Expenses**. Buy a zippered pouch and folder inserts where you can store receipts, repair estimates, letters to and from your insurance company, and a copy of your policy. Create and make a few copies of a **Recovery & Claim Diary** form. (A sample of this form is provided at the end of this chapter.) Put the diary pages in the front of your binder, and write in them daily.

Use the Recovery & Claim Diary and binder to keep track of your recovery, especially your insurance claim. Take notes of all conversations with company representatives and repair professionals. Note when something important is agreed to or when an issue comes up that needs further action. Write down the names or initials and phone numbers of people you speak with and the date you spoke with them. As soon as an adjuster is assigned to your claim, get his or her supervisor's name and contact information. Confirm agreements, disputes, and deadlines in writing via letter, fax, or e-mail. Print out copies of e-mails and keep them in your binder.

This may seem like a waste of time, but it isn't. This advice comes directly from homeowners who've survived a catastrophic loss and recovered. Keeping track of communications with your insurance company is really critical because you will probably have to deal with many different claim handlers. Along the way, each handler may need an entire summary of the steps you have taken up to that point and the Recovery & Claim Diary will help in that process.

If your property is uninhabitable, keep all receipts for temporary/additional living expenses and items you replace. Make sure to submit them to your insurer for reimbursement, and follow up to make sure you're paid in full.

Start with a positive attitude toward the adjuster assigned to your claim, but always find out the supervisor's name and contact information in case you need to go to a higher authority. Putting things in writing helps to keep an insurance claim on track. Writing short and to-the-point letters to your adjuster and his or her superior is an effective way of minimizing delays and communication problems.

Adjusters rotate after disasters, so if you're in a post-disaster area you'll probably get a string of people with varying levels of training and expertise assigned to you. This can be very frustrating, and the best way to stay on track is to keep good notes in your claim diary of what's been agreed to and what's still being worked out.

▶ **Be polite but assertive.**

Your insurance company cashed your premium payment checks in return for promising you three things: **peace of mind, loss reimbursement**, and **prompt claim service**. Your contract with your insurer entitles you to all three of these things. Your rights under the contract are protected under the laws of your state. *Give your insurance company the chance to fulfill its promises and to do right by you, but don't be a pushover. Approach insurance company personnel with a positive and polite attitude, but be assertive.*

▶ **Temporary living expense benefits can be called "ALE" or "Loss of Use."**

Additional Living Expense ("ALE," sometimes called "Loss of Use") benefits cover expenses due to the temporary loss of use of all or part of your home. They entitle you to maintain your standard of living. This means that if your home is uninhabitable and has three bedrooms, your ALE benefits cover rent for a three-bedroom home.

Most policies contain this coverage. Policies vary on the dollar amounts you can claim and how long your ALE benefits will be paid. Some policies contain a set amount of ALE benefits (i.e., $15,000). Others contain ALE limits that are a percentage of the dwelling limits (i.e., 10%). Most policies have a time limit on how long the benefits are payable after a loss. Twelve months was standard. Twenty-four months is becoming more common.

Submit for reimbursement all receipts of meals, lodging, and purchases from the time of the loss until your home is repaired or rebuilt and can be lived in again. Keep copies for your records. *If insurance company delays or circumstances beyond your control make rebuilding or repairs take longer, argue for ALE benefits above your policy limits.*

If the destroyed home was your vacation or weekend home, you are entitled to compensation for temporary replacement quarters until rebuilding is complete. Establish the fair rental value of your home by working with a qualified realtor.

▶ **If the insurance adjuster tells you the damage is not covered or does not exceed your deductible, get an independent opinion.**

The adjuster sent by your insurance company to inspect your home may be new on the job. He or she may not know how to look for and identify all damage and may give you wrong information about what's covered and what's not. Do not blindly trust your adjuster, especially if he or she tells you that no benefits are owed or that the damage does not exceed your deductible. Your home is simply too valuable for you to rely on one person's opinion.

▶ **Find out about coverage basics: Exclusions and delusions.**

Once you've done the math and calculated the dollar limits in your policy, your next challenge is to read and get a basic understanding of what's covered and what's excluded.

An insurance policy is a contract between you and the insurance company. The policy contract gives both you and the insurance company **rights** and **duties**. You have the right to be paid promptly and in full under the terms of the contract. The insurer has the right to require you to submit sufficient proof. You have the duty to cooperate with the insurance company. The insurance company has the duty to treat you fairly and to honor its promises.

Contracts are legal documents, and the words in them are critical. Ask anyone whose home has been seriously damaged, and they'll confirm this statement: A few words in an insurance policy can make all the difference as to whether or not you collect enough benefits to repair or replace your damaged home.

The insurance company wrote the contract, so they have most of the say-so over what's covered and what's not. But remember, **laws trump contracts**. The law is the final word on how the words in a contract are understood and enforced. Laws that dictate how contracts are to be read and enforced often come into play during the insurance claim process for two reasons. The first reason is that the words in an insurance policy are critically important because they determine what is covered and what is excluded. The second reason contract law often comes into play during the claim process is that insurance policies are written by insurance company lawyers and contain technical terms that are unfamiliar to the average person. Contract laws often come into play to resolve disputes between insurers and insureds over what the words in the policy mean. You don't need to hire or be a lawyer to understand the basic contract laws that most often come into play.

One of them is a long-standing legal principle known by the Latin phrase *contra proferentum*. The words in a contract will be construed (interpreted) against the person who wrote (drafted) the contract. Under this principle you, the insured, should win a dispute over the meaning of words in the contract as long as your position is reasonable. If a dispute arises between you and your insurance company over how much they owe for a specific item, it should be resolved in your favor as long as your interpretation of the wording in the contract as to the amount you're entitled to recover for that item is reasonable.

A second legal principle that often comes into play to resolve claim disputes relates to the basic purpose of insurance. This principle is described in legalese as "indemnity in case of loss should be effectuated where possible." In plain English this means that the purpose of insurance is to cover losses, so if the policy can be reasonably read in such a way as to cover a loss, the loss is covered.

The words in the contract are very important, but so are the promises your insurance company made when they sold you the policy. What all this means is simply that although a word in an insurance contract is very important, it is not necessarily *the last word*. Insurance contracts should be required to be written in plain and clear English, but they're not. For that reason, property owners who suffer major damage very often need legal help to resolve insurance disputes.

In an ideal world, no one would need to hire a lawyer to get an insurance claim settled fairly. In *this* world, many do. Most modern insurance policies are half an inch thick and full of exclusions, legalese, and twisted wording. They confound even the most experienced judges. All you can do is take your best shot at understanding your policy, and don't be intimidated by your adjuster. They are very often bluffing!

If you don't have the coverage you were promised or that you need, you're "underinsured." It may be the fault of an agent who advised you against buying flood coverage, or you may have refused an agent's recommendation. If you're very underinsured, you need to get educated on your options for getting the dollars you need to repair or replace your property. Reading articles at the United Policyholders Web site on "underinsurance" is a good way to start.

Your ability to get an agent or insurance company to admit they made a mistake and pony up more than the amounts stated in your policy depends on **available**, **credible evidence** of what was said when you bought the policy; **documents** such as sales brochures, letters, faxes, and e-mails; the **applicable law** in your state about an agent or insurer's duties in connection with setting policy limits; **your willingness to push** to get a fair resolution; and the **effectiveness of your attorney's negotiating and legal skills**.

▶ **The difference between "replacement cost" and "actual cash value" coverage affects how much you'll be paid and when you'll get the money.**

Many homeowners' policies have a feature that increases your coverage above the limits stated on the "declarations page" under certain conditions. These are called "extended replacement" or "guaranteed replacement" policies. The increases come via add-ons to the policy called "endorsements." Your agent or insurer should have offered you the added protection of an extended replacement cost endorsement when he or she sold you the policy because underinsurance has become such a common problem after disasters that all agents and insurers should be aware of it and take steps to be sure their customers are safely covered.

Other policies simply have set limits (i.e., "replacement cost up to policy limits" or "actual cash value"). Nearly all policies have inflation guard provisions that automatically increase your limits over time. Insurers generally promise that these provisions keep policy limits adequate by adjusting them in step with inflation. Many large loss victims report that the inflation guard feature of their policies failed to keep limits in step with current costs and left them far short of what they needed to recover.

Policies generally exclude the cost of improvements over what you had prior to a loss, even if law requires them. Most policies sold today contain what's called a "building code" or "ordinance coverage" endorsement that protects you from having to pay out of pocket for legally required improvements to your property.

Here are the most common forms of property policies:

☞ **Replacement Coverage (RC)** is what most people today have for their dwellings and their possessions. It allows you to replace what you lost at today's prices regardless of how you got the items, what condition they were in, or what you paid for them. However, depreciation will be applied to many items even under a replacement policy (see below re: "**Actual Cash Value**" and "**Depreciation**"), up to the limits stated on your declarations page.

☞ **Extended Replacement Coverage (ERC)** allows you to replace what you lost at today's prices, even if the cost exceeds the limits stated on your Dec page, up to a set extended percentage limit. **Example:** You have $200,000 limits on your dwelling and a 25% extended replacement cost endorsement. This means that you have up to $250,000 to rebuild, provided that a reliable contractor estimates that it will cost at least $250,000 and that you are successful in negotiating your structural settlement with your insurance company for at least $250,000.

☞ **Guaranteed Replacement Coverage (GRC)** requires your insurer to cover the full cost of replacing your home, regardless of the limits stated in your policy. This type of policy used to be widely available but was discontinued by virtually all insurers after 1992.

☞ **Actual Cash Value (ACV)** is sometimes also called "Fair Market Value," which is the amount a willing buyer would have paid a willing seller for destroyed property just prior to the destruction. Insurers like to calculate ACV as replacement cost minus depreciation. Many items in your claim will be settled on the basis of their ACV. Insurers often confuse their claimants and are inconsistent in the way that they calculate and deduct depreciation.

▶ **It is important for you to understand common exclusions and the phrases "like kind and quality," "uniform and consistent appearance," and "line of sight."**

In general, your insurer should "make you whole" by paying what it will cost to repair or replace damaged items, subject to the law and the terms and conditions of the policy contract. The basic idea of insurance is to put you back in the same position where you were before a loss. For most property owners, their home is their biggest asset. They want to protect the value of that asset, so they buy insurance.

One industry leader advertises its policies with the tagline, "We get you back where you belong" and has been running a television commercial that plays on that theme for many years. The commercial shows a house burning, then rewinds the tape to show it good as new again. The message is consistent with the expectations most property owners have when they pay premiums in return for peace of mind. Insured property owners expect that if they suffer a loss, their insurer will put them back where they were before the loss.

These days, however, insurers are selling policies that are more like Swiss cheese than a blanket that fully covers you. If you're working on getting paid fairly to repair major property damage, you're certain to run up against an exclusion you didn't expect. Exclusions for certain types of water and earth movement damage, war, earthquakes, neglect, and pollution are commonly found in property policies. The wording of policies differs, and things get complicated when you have a large claim.

Traditional insurance covers the cost of replacing damaged or destroyed items with items of "**like kind and quality**." If your solid wood door is damaged beyond repair, your insurance covers the cost of a new solid wood door. If your home had lathe and plaster walls that are damaged beyond repair, you're entitled to the cost of replacing them with lathe and plaster if you so choose. This is consistent with the basic idea that insurance puts you back where you were before a loss. Getting paid for "like kind and quality" versus "equivalent construction" makes a big difference if you have an older home. To preserve its value and integrity you'll want like kind and quality repairs.

Recently, some insurers began cutting corners by selling policies containing a new, lower standard of dwelling coverage. **"Equivalent Construction" Limited Dwelling Coverage** is a relatively new type of policy sold by only a few companies. Instead of paying benefits to replace damaged or destroyed items with "like kind and quality," these policies allow the insurer to pay for what it deems "equivalent" items. This means that if your solid door was destroyed, the insurer may say it only owes for a hollow door. If you had lathe and plaster, the insurer may say it only owes for sheetrock. A policy that contains "equivalent construction" language, instead of "like kind and quality," allows an insurer to pay for cheaper materials and shortcut repair methods.

Disputes are likely to arise if you have one of these newer policies with lesser coverage. So if you have one, make sure it was clearly explained to you by the sales agent and that you were charged less for it than you would have paid for a traditional replacement cost policy.

Traditional insurance pays to return your property to a "**uniform and consistent appearance**." Disputes very often arise in partial loss situations over whether the insurer will replace, for example, a whole roof when only part has been damaged, or a whole wall of siding when only part has been damaged. Property owners don't want their most valuable asset to look like a patchwork with different colored roof tiles, shingles or paint colors. Insurers don't want to pay a nickel more than they have to, so they often pay only for the damaged portion of something even though it is impractical to replace or repair only that damaged portion. This means the property owner has to fight for a fair settlement so that their property will have a uniform and consistent appearance.

"**Line of sight**" is a common phrase that often comes up during the adjustment of a large property damage claim and basically refers to the way your property looks to the naked eye. It relates to the concept of a "uniform and consistent appearance," and, again, you should be working to be paid enough to allow you to return your property to its pre-loss appearance or as close to that pre-loss appearance as is practical under the circumstances.

▶ **Stay in touch with others to share information—there's strength in numbers.**

In addition to keeping up your Recovery & Claim Diary, communicate with your neighbors after an area-wide disaster. Find those people who are also insured with your insurance company and meet with them regularly to share information and ideas on securing a fair settlement. There is negotiating power in numbers. There have been many instances where "carrier-specific" support groups of insureds have succeeded in getting their insurance company to agree to extend deadlines and make other concessions "across-the-board" following large-scale disasters.

Work with neighbors and friends who've lost property to find out what they're being told by insurance adjusters and claim professionals. Experience has clearly shown that united, educated policyholders get faster, fairer settlements. Network and communicate with others who are recovering and insured with the same company you are. You'll be glad you did.

▶ **Be an assertive claimant.**

If your adjuster is rude, unreasonable, or hard to reach, complain in writing to his or her superiors. If your insurer is taking unreasonably long to process your claim, send written demands for action that contain specific deadlines. (i.e., "Please respond within 10 business days from the date of this letter.") Use your Recovery & Claim Diary as the paper trail that supports your position.

If need be, complain all the way up the corporate ladder to the top executive of the insurance company and register a complaint with the agency in your state that regulates insurance companies. If you feel your claim is not being handled fairly, contact a qualified attorney or public adjuster who specializes in representing policyholders.

▶ **Cooperate with your insurer, but do not give recorded or sworn statements or sign away any rights without legal advice.**

The best way to get paid fairly and promptly on a claim is to prepare detailed, accurate lists, photos and whatever proof you can gather; then submit everything to your insurer with a dated cover letter that sets a reasonable deadline for their payment in full or at least a response. Because some people "pad" their insurance claims or claim items they didn't actually have, insurance companies require proof before they will pay.

Your insurance policy and the laws in your state spell out your duty to cooperate and the insurer's right to require proof of your claim. You must cooperate with reasonable requests for information from your insurance company that relate to your claim. This includes answering questions, allowing the adjuster to inspect your property, and submitting written proof. In addition to asking questions, inspecting your property, and requiring you to submit written proof, your insurer has the right to ask you to give a "recorded statement" and to submit to an "examination under oath (EUO)" to prove you truly had what you are claiming.

If your insurance company has unanswered questions about items in your claim and asks you to give a recorded statement or be examined under oath (usually by a lawyer), they must be reasonable. They cannot legally grill you for hours on end on unrelated subjects or insist that you show up at an inconvenient place or at an inconvenient time. Use your own tape recorder to record your statement and the insurer's questions. Don't be intimidated. Small mistakes on claim forms are very common, especially with large losses, and you can correct them without a penalty. Just be honest.

If your insurer demands a recorded statement or an examination under oath, it makes sense for you to check with a lawyer first. If there are any possible legal issues or coverage disputes involved in your claim, it's important to avoid saying things, even unknowingly, that may hurt you. Making a mistake on tape or signing documents in a rush will reduce your ability to fully recover the policy benefits you need to repair or replace your property.

Note: You are not obligated to give your insurer copies of tax returns to prove you had the financial means to have owned the destroyed items you're claiming. If your insurer is challenging the accuracy of items you're claiming, gather and submit as much proof as you can locate.

▶ **Do not submit a claim form that says "Final" or "Full" until you are sure you understand your rights, your coverage, and the full extent of your damage and the reimbursement you're claiming.**

Your claim may take longer to settle fairly than you'd anticipated. Lots of new terms and information will be thrown at you. It's important to pace yourself, keep learning, and get help when you need it. Don't let insurance company adjusters rush you into a quick settlement. The check they are offering may seem like a lot of money, but the amount may be far below what you are entitled to recover. It takes time to calculate what the insurance company owes you after a large loss. An adjuster who tries to rush you into a settlement may be trying to earn brownie points with the boss by underpaying and closing your claim quickly. He or she may also suspect that you are under-insured—that your policy limits are too low to fully cover your losses.

Read all checks and drafts on both sides before depositing or cashing them. Don't accept any checks with words like "full" or "final settlement" printed on them. You should not have to sign a release to collect your insurance benefits. If your insurer wants you to sign a release, find out why. Be very cautious about sign-ing away your rights.

If there is no dispute over whether or not your claim is cov-ered, there is no legitimate reason for your insurance company to ask you to sign a "waiver" or "release" form in exchange for payments. They owe you money under your insurance policy contract. The proof of loss forms you've submitted and the checks they issue you should be sufficient receipts for their records. However, sometimes an insurance company representa-tive will ask you to sign a "waiver" or "release" form before they'll pay the money they owe you. "Waivers" and "release" forms are legal documents that cut off your rights to make a further claim for policy benefits. They release your insurer from any further responsibility on your claim.

Hidden damage and expenses often crop up during repairs, and many property owners end up submitting supplemental claims. A signed waiver or release will make that difficult or impossible for you. So if your insurer asks you to sign docu-ments other than basic claim forms or proofs of loss, do not sign them without first getting advice from an experienced attorney.

▶ **Contact your state insurance regulator if you think you're not getting fair treatment. File a formal com-plaint and follow up on it.**

Every state has an agency that regulates insurance companies and laws on how insurance companies are supposed to handle claims. If your insurance company is treating you unfairly and you've gone as far as you can with them but still can't solve the problem, your next step should be to file a complaint with the insurance regulatory agency in your state and take advantage of whatever information and services they offer to resolve claim problems. Even if they don't solve your problem, you've let them know there are problems that need attention.

A "commissioner" or regulator, who has two basic jobs, heads every state agency that regulates insurance companies. The first job is to watch over the finances of insurance companies doing business in the state to make sure they have enough money to pay claims. The second job is to make sure insurers are selling decent products and treating their customers fairly.

A commissioner who leans on insurers to treat customers fairly is a big help. State insurance commissioners who don't lean hard enough sometimes need to be pressured to do so, so let them know you need their help.

Don't be afraid that complaining will make matters worse by angering your insurance company. It has the opposite effect. Once your insurer knows you're not a pushover, their conduct usually improves. When it comes to insurance claims, "the squeaky wheel gets the grease."

▶ **Get professional help if and when you need it, and check references and licenses very carefully.**

You may decide that you want to hire professional help to take over the time-consuming details of documenting a major or total loss and negotiating on your behalf with the insurer to recover your full contents benefits.

Dealing with a large insurance claim on top of the emotional upset from a catastrophic loss is a big job. Many people—particularly working people, single parents, and disabled or elderly claimants—find that they are unable to put in the time and effort it takes to settle a total loss claim. Others feel the deck is stacked against them and want to even the odds of getting a fair settlement by bringing in professional help.

Whatever your reasons are, if you decide to get help, make sure that you hire a reputable professional whose license is in good standing and whose references check out. Do not hire any professional to represent you in negotiating a settlement with your insurance company unless you have personally talked to *at least two, preferably three or more prior clients* who were satisfied with the way the professional handed their insurance claims.

Two types of professionals can help you get a fair settlement of a large contents claim: **public adjusters** and **attorneys** who have hands-on insurance claim experience. There are also "independent" adjusters, but in most states they work only for insurance companies who need extra adjusting staff—not for policyholders.

▶ **Don't feel pressured to hire a public adjuster or lawyer prematurely. But if you need one, make sure he or she has hands-on experience representing "insureds" in claim disputes.**

As a person who paid premiums in return for insurance protection—you're known in the legal world as "the insured." Another term for "the insured" is "policyholder." Remember, you paid for insurance protection *and* good claim service. You should not have to hire and pay a professional to help you collect your insurance benefits, but the sad truth is that many property owners who suffer large losses end up needing professional and legal help to get a fair settlement. You can guess why—it's all about money. And another thing—if your insurance company brings in a lawyer, as they often do, you should too. Insurance coverage and claim disputes require specialized knowledge of the law. Don't expect a real estate or family lawyer to have that knowledge.

Policyholder attorneys will help you if your claim is being unfairly denied or if you are being mistreated by your insurer via "lowball" settlement offers, delays, or other unfair claim practices. As with any professional, check references and professional standing before you retain counsel.

▶ **Paying for professional claim help on an hourly basis can get costly fast.**

Handling the details of a major insured loss and "wrangling" with an insurance company can be very time-consuming. If you agree to pay an attorney or public adjuster by the hour to handle your claim, you will run up a big bill mighty fast.

Where state law allows it, public adjusters and policyholder attorneys will work for you on a percentage or contingent fee arrangement. This means that their fee comes out of monies they obtain for you from the insurance company. Professional fees are always negotiable. Percentage/contingent fee agreements allow you affordable access to professional help, but they will affect the amount of your net recovery. If the professional you hire does his or her job correctly, you will likely get more money than you would have gotten on your own even after the fee is subtracted.

For more detailed tips on the pros and cons of hiring a public adjuster or attorney, please visit United Policyholders' Web site: www.uphelp.org

Recovery & Claim Diary

(Sample)

DATE   **NOTES**

Chapter 3

How to Inventory and Get Paid Fairly

for Your Damaged or Destroyed Personal Property / Contents Items

The **Contents** part of your home insurance is a broad category that includes everything that's not a part of the dwelling structure. Furniture, clothing, and kitchenware are only a few of the many items in a typical home.

As you learned in Chapter 1, "**Steps on the Road to Recovery: What Disaster Survivors Need to Know**," dealing with your contents claim can be the most emotionally difficult part of the insurance recovery process. Most loss victims find it very painful to sit down and try to remember each item they lost, and many find it impossible. Some insurance company adjusters require more "hoop-jumping," "t-crossing," and "i-dotting" than others. Creating a contents inventory list to submit to an insurance company and negotiating the fair replacement cost of damaged and destroyed items is a very time-consuming and challenging process.

▶ **You may or may not have enough insurance coverage to repair and replace everything that was damaged, but you can maximize your insurance recovery and save your sanity by using the lists and tips in this book.**

Your goal is to collect the full amount that your insurer owes you, which in some cases will be the full amount of your contents insurance limits. If it is clear that everything you had is gone, try negotiating with your insurer to cut a check for your full contents limits (or slightly less) without requiring you to prepare an itemized list. (See the **Negotiation Tips** section in this chapter).

However, to get a fair contents settlement, you will probably need to put the time and effort into listing and pricing everything you lost and submitting receipts as you replace items. Use lists, photos, family, and friends to help you remember and write down a complete inventory of all damaged and destroyed items. Use stores and the Internet to set a value for every lost item and the cost to replace it.

Don't claim items you didn't have or exaggerate values. Insurance fraud is a felony and even a small misrepresentation can cause you big headaches.

The following tips reflect the best advice from many survivors' personal experiences as they recovered from large losses. It is their hope that future survivors will benefit from this book, the hard lessons they learned, and new technologies that make it easier to reconstruct the contents of a typical home.

▶ **Do your best to read your complete policy and figure out how much coverage you have for repairing and replacing contents.**

As explained in chapter 2, the declarations page lists your name and address, policy number, dollar amounts of coverage and "endorsement" codes. The policy will be hard to read and understand, but knowing what you're covered for is a critical first step in the claim process.

When reading your policy, start with the declarations page and check the dollar amounts and limits for your **Contents/ Personal Property** (normally, *Coverage C*). In addition to the dollar amounts on the Dec page, there may be limits in other parts of the policy for specific items, such as valuable papers, artwork, computers, and so on.

You will need to do some math and piecing together to figure out what your policy limits actually are. Basic contents limits are generally set by the insurance company as a percentage of your dwelling coverage limits (Coverage A).

Normally, Coverage C (Contents) is set at 75% of the Coverage A limits. Check your limits for "scheduled" personal property items (i.e., artwork, jewelry, and valuables). Make sure that the policy covers what you think you bought and what the agent/insurer told you it would cover. Many homeowners who experience a total loss are underinsured, meaning that they don't have sufficient limits to cover the cost of replacing what they had. If you find you are underinsured, research your options. This may start with a call to your agent.

If either your insurance agent or insurance company drags its feet, call the consumer services department at your state insurance regulator's office and tell them you need immediate help.

▶ **Learn about three terms that affect the amount of your contents claim recovery.**

Actual cash value (ACV). ACV is the "old" price of an item as it was pre-loss, sometimes explained as the price a willing buyer would have paid you immediately before the event that caused your loss.

The "normal" process for submitting and getting paid on the contents part of your insurance claim is as follows: The claimant (with help from the insurance company adjuster) prepares a detailed list of every single damaged or destroyed item, noting approximate age, value, and replacement cost. The adjuster/insurer depreciates certain items to account for their age and cuts a check for what's called the *Actual Cash Value* of the entire inventory.

Some policies limit payouts to ACV, and that's all they pay. If you've got an ACV policy, you'll probably need to argue for less depreciation to be taken on major Items. But once the check is cut, that's all you'll get, regardless of what it costs to actually replace what you had.

Replacement cost (RC). Most policies these days are replacement cost (RC) policies because they're supposed to cover the cost of replacing what you've lost. RC is the *new* price of what it would cost to replace an item. To collect the full amount you're entitled to under an RC policy, you have to replace the items and send the receipts to the insurer with a demand for the balance they owe you. Insurers don't volunteer to pay. You must insist on it!

Note: Disaster survivors are often able to negotiate waivers of certain policy requirements with their insurance companies. Many property owners have been successful in getting insurers to pay projected replacement costs prior to actual replacement following government declared disasters.

Depreciation. This is the loss in value from all causes, including age, wear, and tear. Your adjuster/insurer will depreciate certain items (pay you less than their true replacement cost) before paying you for their ACV.

▶ **Give the insurance company enough documentation so they know what you had and how much it will cost to replace or repair it.**

Most insurance companies have inventory forms that they want claimants to use to list and value their destroyed or damaged items. Some insurance companies have several versions of inventory forms that require different levels of detail, and it's the luck of the draw as to which form your adjuster gives you. If you're lucky, your insurer will accept a contents claim inventory form without a microscopic level of detail. If you're not so lucky, your insurer will "nitpick" and make you list and describe every item and research the true current replacement cost. Bathroom items are a perfect example: It makes common sense for an insurer to allow a claimant to group medicine cabinet items instead of listing every single Q-tip or bar of soap.

Check with your insurer to see if they'll accept your contents inventory in the form of a computer list that you create yourself. This list can mimic the insurance company's forms, but it will be far easier for you to create and finalize than a hard copy document from the insurance company. An inventory list you create on your computer can be modified as you go along.

You **are not obligated** to produce purchase receipts for damaged or destroyed items or to prove you had the means to buy them. You **are obligated** to provide reasonable proof of what you had and how much it is going to cost to replace or repair it. If your insurer is hassling you by requiring an unreasonable amount of detail, and if your efforts to fix the problem via letters and phone calls up the authority chain have failed, file a complaint with your state insurance regulator and/or hire professional help.

Negotiation Tips

▶ **Every disaster and loss has unique circumstances. Find the path that works best for you.**

"Normal" rules may not apply to large damage claims or claims related to large-scale natural disasters. Think outside the box.

Before you even start the painful process of sitting down to list every single item that was in the home that you may have lived in your entire adult life, remember this word: **Negotiation**.

If everything you had was destroyed, it is logical that you are entitled to be paid your full contents policy limits. This is true, especially where you followed your agent or insurer's recommendations on coverage limits. But to prevent fraud, insurers generally require that every claimant—even those who've lost everything—fully document their losses to get paid in full. The key word here is *generally*. There are always exceptions, and here's an important tip:

Some insurance companies will waive the inventory requirement if you give them good reasons to do so and if you negotiate. If you have good reasons, there's no harm in asking your adjuster and insurance company to waive the inventory requirement and pay your limits. But you should know that this is a long shot. Insurers only relax the rules when they feel they really have to.

▶ **Disaster survivors have successfully argued as follows:**

"I followed your recommendations on how much contents coverage to buy, but I'm close to my limit and I'm only half way through completing my inventory. I shouldn't have to keep going—it's upsetting and a waste of time. Please cut me a check for my full limits without further documentation."

"The claim process has been a second nightmare so far. To avoid the further trauma of sitting down to describe all the cherished things I lost, I'll accept 90% of my policy limits for contents—less than you owe me— to save time for me and for your company. I've lost everything. Please make this practical business decision."

Make your request in writing to your insurer, and even if your adjuster says "no" right off the bat, go over his or her head before you give up.

▶ **Make use of existing lists after you have made your own list as explained in Chapter 1, and enlist the help of friends and relatives to help you complete your inventory.**

Preparing a contents inventory to prove your claim can be extremely time consuming. Take advantage of what has worked for other disaster survivors in recent years:

Sitting down and recalling the contents room by room, closet by closet, shelf by shelf, is the best way to get started. Your home had unique items. You need to remember them. But your home also had items that are commonly found in many homes. You are likely to have forgotten many of them. *After* you have exhausted your memory, make use of existing lists to help you remember more common items. Begin with the comprehensive lists in the **Household Inventory Guide** chapters of this book. You can also find a sample personal property inventory list in the Claim Tips section of **www.uphelp.org**.

Many people ask how they can help after a catastrophic loss. Because completing your inventory can be emotionally draining, enlist friends and family to help. They can save you time and can be a valuable source of emotional support. For instance, give a friend a discreet list of items that need to be researched, valued, and documented (i.e., china and silverware patterns). Also, friends and family may have photos that were taken inside your home that will help jog your memory and serve as proof for your insurer.

▶ **Take advantage of time-saving technology when documenting all the things you lost.**

At some point you will need to assign prices to the items that you list in your inventory. **Many stores have gift registry scanners that can help.** You can walk around the store with the scanner and use it to compile a list that describes and prices the items that were destroyed. The printout can be supplemented with additional items and submitted directly to your adjuster/insurer.

Take advantage of **Internet shopping/pricing information.** With the widespread use of Internet research, valuing and pricing lost items and replacement costs can now be a few simple keystrokes away.

▶ **The better you are able to document destroyed and damaged property and the cost of replacement and repairs, the better your insurance settlement will be.**

In most cases, written or photographic proof of destroyed items will also have been destroyed in a fire or other disaster. Your descriptions of lost items, along with descriptions given by witnesses, family members, neighbors, and friends should suffice, and your company must reimburse you according to your policy.

Credit card companies and retailers may be able to help you reconstruct purchases and identify replacement costs. Public adjusters can help if you are overwhelmed with the prospect of preparing a complete personal property inventory. Get extensions of time from your insurer if you need them.

▶ **Negotiate with the insurer to reduce the amount by which they depreciate items. Don't forget to submit receipts to collect full replacement values.**

Depreciation amounts are subjective and very negotiable. Insurers may use an IRS depreciation schedule or their own schedules. It's often hard to pin down an adjuster on how he or she arrived at the depreciated figures. *Be prepared to fight to get the full amounts you're entitled to, particularly for major items, and don't forget to submit receipts and to collect your full replacement cost value after you replace items.* Ask your insurer to provide you with a copy of the depreciation schedule it uses.

▶ **Negotiate ACV deductions on a case-by-case basis to reflect how worn the items really were.**

For instance, the furniture in your guest room should be depreciated less than the furniture in your master bedroom because it was used less and was in better shape. The replacement cost and the actual cash value of some items are the same.

Many items should not be subject to depreciation. Examples include antiques, fine art and jewelry, computer media (CDs, etc.), software, framing, masonry, concrete, insulation, and light fixtures. Some items depreciate faster than others. For example, electronics, soft furniture, clothes, and shoes depreciate faster than hard furniture, washing machines, dryers, and so on.

You're unlikely to replace everything you lost, and it's a hassle to have to keep providing receipts over time. *Try to maximize your ACV payments by arguing for lower depreciation on big-ticket items and identifying the true replacement cost of items at standard, not discount, retailers.*

▶ **If you hire a public adjuster to handle your contents claim, negotiate a reasonable fee for value added.**

A public adjuster (P.A.) is a licensed insurance claim professional who will work with you to document and value your losses and who will take over negotiating with the insurer to get you a full and fair settlement. A good P.A. saves you time and aggravation and can get you a higher settlement than you would get on your own because they're familiar with insurance lingo and the claim process.

The adjuster assigned to your claim by your insurance company should welcome a reputable P.A. Together they can streamline the process and resolve the claim. If your insurance company adjuster tries to talk you out of hiring a P.A., you should be suspicious. He or she may simply be trying to get away with underpaying your claim.

Be very careful to check references, and read the contract when you hire a P.A. to take over your claim. Get a second opinion on the P.A.'s proposed contract before you sign it. An inexperienced or dishonest P.A. will make a bad situation worse and cost you time and money, so be careful before you sign on the dotted line. P.A.s who take on too many clients after a disaster delay their clients' claims and give insurance companies someone else to blame.

Chapter 4

Dwelling Tips

How to Get a Fair Settlement on Your Damaged or Destroyed Home

Your goal is to collect the full amount your insurer owes you for what it would reasonably cost to repair/rebuild your home. Even if you may not rebuild or are considering doing your own repairs, your insurer still owes you what it could cost to have a professional contractor do the work, subject to your policy limits.

▶ **Here are four specific action steps to take to collect what is owed to you.**

Step one. Document your pre-loss property so that you and the insurance company have a starting point to negotiate a settlement. For instance, how many rooms did your home have? What size were the rooms? How were the rooms finished? What kind of windows did you have in your home?

Use whatever information you can get your hands on to recreate exterior and interior drawings and detailed descriptions of what your property was like before the loss. Building plans, photos, oral descriptions, and whatever's left will help. The information doesn't have to be scientifically exact, but don't exaggerate or "pad."

Step two. Document the amount and type of repairs that need to be done so that you and the insurance company can agree about the work and the quantities and materials that need to be priced.

This is known in the insurance business as a "scope" (i.e., how many feet of flooring need to be replaced, how much paint you need, how much carpeting you need, and so on). If you can agree on a scope of repairs with the insurance company, that scope can be passed on to contractors. The contractors come up with estimates based on the scope. If their prices are far apart, you and the insurance company can see where they differ. Even if there are disagreements over what needs to be done and what's covered, having one document that lays it all out is extremely useful to settling a large insurance claim.

Step three. Get at least two independent estimates from licensed, reputable contractors that you would hire to repair or replace your home. Make sure that they account for the increased costs of materials that follow every disaster. Work toward a settlement with your insurance company that is based on the independent estimates. The insurance company will get its own estimates. Don't accept a settlement that is based on their estimates without getting at least two of your own.

Step four. Negotiate a settlement of your dwelling claim with the insurance company that will cover the true costs of replacing/repairing your damaged property. If they won't budge from a lowball number, consider going to "appraisal" and get professional help.

☞ *Read on for more detailed tips on settling your dwelling claim.*

▶ **Insist on "uniform and consistent" repairs and "like kind and quality" materials. Do not accept "lowball" estimates, substandard workmanship or nonmatching items.**

Insurance companies may pressure you to agree to their contractors' cut-rate repair estimates or short-cut repair methods. The costs of materials go up after a disaster; that's just the way of the world. Most people's homes are their biggest asset, so hold out to find the right repair professional and get the right amount from your insurance company to pay for getting the job done right.

If the adjuster tells you there is no damage to your walls or flooring, get a second opinion. Push for the best inspection methods on your engineer's recommendation. Don't settle for limited testing. (For example, inspecting walls by drilling holes in them is not as good as actually tearing off sections of the wall in areas with suspected damage).

If you have only a partial loss and your adjuster tells you that the insurer won't pay to match paint colors, roof tile materials, or carpeting, argue back. In most states and under most policies you're entitled to be paid for the cost of restoring your property to a uniform and consistent appearance. If you didn't have two-color walls or carpets before the disaster, you don't have to settle for them afterward. If your adjuster tells you that the insurance company doesn't owe to "match" in your state, check around before accepting that statement as true.

▶ **If you're sure you're going to relocate and don't want to rebuild, you still need to determine the cost of replacing or repairing your home to reach a fair claim settlement.**

Even if you're not going to rebuild the same house or rebuild at the same location, you still need to pull together documentation to establish what the costs would be if you were going to rebuild the same house at the same location. That's what your insurer owes you. You're likely to get ripped off or have headaches and disputes if you try to reach a claim settlement based only on plans and estimates for a different size or style of home.

▶ **Always get independent rebuilding and repair estimates from reputable professionals. You do not have to accept the insurance company's contractors or estimates.**

Be skeptical of "lowball" estimates from contractors who have standing relationships with insurance company adjusters. Get written estimates of the true costs of replacing or repairing your home from reputable, independent professionals that you would hire to do the actual work. If you do not intend to rebuild the exact same house, you are still entitled to settle your claim on the basis of estimates to replace what you had. To ensure a fair settlement, get contractors' estimates on the original plans for your home. If the original plans don't exist, it's worthwhile to pay to get "as-built" drawings of your former home.

▶ **Insist that your claim be settled for the amount of a reasonable contractor's estimate. You do not have to accept the insurance company's contractor or computer-generated estimates.**

Check with your local building department and use word-of-mouth to find reputable contractors who have experience repairing severe catastrophic damage and doing total rebuilds. If you were in an area-wide disaster, local contractors will be in high demand and short supply. Before you hire contractors, check their references and their standings with your State Board of Contractors. If a contractor says his or her work is bonded, verify that by asking to see a copy of that person's policy. In additional to having a healthy skepticism of relationships between insurance company adjusters and contractors, you should be aware of the following:

- Avoid out-of-state, inexperienced, or unreliable contractors without proper insurance of their own.
- If the event that caused the damage made pre-existing damage worse, you should be covered for the necessary repairs.
- Watch for hidden damage, especially in walls and floors. Wet and mildewed areas can be potentially hazardous. For instance, monitor your air after any flood, especially if you smell mold, mildew, or musky odors. You may have to fight to get the full amount of policy benefits you paid for.
- Don't be penny-wise and pound-foolish by refusing to pay experts to advise you on the scope of damage and cost of repairs. They will help you prove your claim.

▶ **Work toward an agreed "scope of loss" with your insurer.**

The best tool for getting a fair settlement to repair or replace your home is a good "scope of loss." A scope of loss is a document that describes in detail the home you will be replacing/repairing. An accurate scope of loss goes room by room, listing the quantities and qualities of each feature and component. A scope of loss should be prepared without prices so competing contractors can add their own prices and their estimates can be compared, apples to apples.

The insurance company adjuster or your own contractor or public adjuster can prepare a draft scope of loss. A good scope needs to be reviewed thoroughly to make sure it's complete and accurate. For an example of a detailed scope of loss, see United Policyholders' Sample Scope of Loss. A good scope of loss should contain most or all of the items listed in Trade Summary Breakdown in the Claim Tips section of **www.uphelp.org**.

▶ **Get your contractors and the insurer's contractors to bid on the same "scope of loss."**

Most claim disputes arise because the insurer's and the insured's repair estimates are thousands of dollars apart and cannot be reconciled because they're not based on the same scope of loss.

☞ *If you and your insurance company can reach agreement on a detailed scope of loss, you can proceed to have your contractor(s) and theirs bid on the scope and you will be on the right path to a fair claim settlement.*

▶ **Do not be pressured into a quick settlement.**

Your adjuster may try to rush you into a fast settlement. Settling fast almost always means you're settling low. An insurance claim settlement is a negotiation. It's important to understand the motivation of the person on the side of the negotiation. You should recognize some reasons why your adjuster may pressure you to accept a quick settlement.

Most adjusters are juggling more files than they can handle, and they do what they can to reduce their workload. Adjusters get favorable performance reviews for closing files quickly and minimizing payouts. Favorable performance reviews garner bonuses or salary increases.

Another reason your adjuster may rush you is to avoid having to deal with potential complications he or she sees relating to the damage and/or your coverage. Mold is a perfect example. If a trained adjuster sees signs of mold that you don't see and knows there's a new exclusion in your policy that will bar coverage for mold cleanup—he or she may rush you to settle before you notice the signs and challenge the insurance company's refusal to pay for the cleanup.

One more reason your adjuster may try to rush you is that he or she is not properly trained to take all the damage into account when handing an insurance claim. Especially after catastrophes, some companies hire adjusters who have no prior insurance industry experience. The person assigned to adjust your claim may not be trained or even knowledgeable about the coverages and policy provisions at issue. He or she may tell you that the damage was present before (pre-existed) the event. Don't be railroaded. Documenting a major loss to ensure a full, fair recovery requires work. Before you know the true amount of your insurance claim, you must get estimates from reputable contractors and inventory all lost or damaged possessions. This takes time. Damage to a structure should be fully inspected by licensed professionals who are qualified to tell you the scope and costs of necessary repairs.

▶ **Make sure to have your home properly inspected by reputable professionals experienced in hazardous materials abatement and in detecting hidden damage.**

Your insurer generally owes for proper clean up and removal of hazardous materials and, also, to repair all damage, including what may not be obvious to the naked eye. Adjusters very often overlook or fail to pay for the "abatement" of damaged asbestos, insulation materials, mold growth, and damage hidden behind walls and under floors.

Earthquakes and water have an impact on hidden areas. Mold, mildew, and fungus may grow inside walls and ducts. Foundations and support beams may sustain cracks. Protect your property and your family's health by making sure your home is fully inspected by qualified professionals, and hire an environmental hygienist to inspect and test the air inside your home prior to moving back in after repairs or reconstruction is complete.

Chapter 5

Frequently Asked Questions About Insurance Issues

Q ▪ *My insurance company's representatives are telling me that the damage to my home is excluded/not covered. Are they right?*

A ▪ Coverage questions are rarely black and white. The best way to get answers is by educating yourself. The factors that determine coverage include:

- ▪ **Causation:** The cause(s) of the damage and the condition of your home prior to the loss.

- ▪ **Words:** The specific wording of the exclusions or limitations your insurer is relying on to deny your claim.

- ▪ **Laws:** The laws in your state relating to insurance claims, contracts, and unfair business practices.

- ▪ **Politics:** Whether or not your elected and appointed public officials will put pressure on insurers to pay fairly and promptly.

- ▪ **You:** Your willingness to take whatever steps you need to take to make your insurance company fulfill the promises they made to you and to meet their obligations under the laws of your state.

There are many reasons why the adjuster may be wrong when he or she tells you the insurer doesn't owe you benefits.

Q ▪ *My adjuster seems friendly and knowledgeable. Why would he or she mislead me?*

A ▪ Insurance companies are profit-making businesses, and their employees are not social workers. Their goal is to close your claim quickly and without paying a dime more than necessary. *Your adjuster may be friendly, but he or she is not your friend.*

Insurance companies naturally try to control their payouts, especially after large-scale catastrophes. There is a lot of confusing wording and legalese in insurance contracts, and this wording helps them to **limit** their payouts, but there are laws to protect you.

Q ▪ *What approach should I take to get a fair claim settlement?*

A ▪ If you're like most people, your home is your biggest asset. Insurance companies often read their policies with a bias that is too much in their own favor and against your interests. Don't accept an insurance company's rejection of your claim without getting other opinions on the causes of the damage and the wording of the exclusion. You paid good money for insurance protection.

Do your best to settle your claim directly with your adjuster by following United Policyholders' tips to get your insurer to honor its promises. If you feel you've tried everything and haven't succeeded, hire a qualified attorney or a reputable public adjuster.

Insurance policies are contracts written by insurance company lawyers. Doesn't it make sense to get legal advice for yourself before taking the insurance company's word that you're not covered? Your goal is to be effective in claim settlement negotiations. Legal arguments can really strengthen your negotiating position. You can consult with a lawyer to discuss the situation and develop a strategy, then use his or her advice and arguments to convince your insurance company to change its position without getting involved in a lawsuit.

Mediation and informal settlement negotiations can be the fastest and least expensive way to resolve insurance claim disputes. Having your own lawyer involved means the scales won't be tipped so heavily in the insurance company's favor. Just make sure the lawyer you hire is qualified and skilled. The right lawyer will make your life a whole lot easier, and the wrong one will have the opposite effect. Most lawsuits are resolved informally before trial, but even if yours doesn't, the civil litigation process truly works and is a very important part of our democratic system.

Q ▪ *I don't want to get involved in a lawsuit. Isn't there something else I can do?*

A ▪ Yes. Use your insurance **Recovery & Claim Diary** to create a record of everything that's happened between you and the insurance company. Write short and to-the-point letters to your adjuster. Outline issues that need to be resolved and problems that are delaying the settlement of your claim. Always include a reasonable deadline that tells the insurance company when you expect a reply (i.e., "Please respond no later than 14 business days from the date on this letter).

Write letters to your adjusters' supervisors, their supervisors, and even to the president or CEO of the insurance company. Follow up with phone calls. Take the time to read the wording of the specific exclusions or limitations that the insurance company is relying on. Make sure to read the whole policy and whatever brochures or sales materials you can get your hands on. You may find words that show that they promised or owe more benefits than they're offering.

If you were in an area-wide disaster that also had an impact on your neighbors, be sure to share information, problems, and solutions with them. Follow UP's claim tips by keeping a **Recovery & Claim Diary**, staying organized, writing to higher-ups in the company, and getting help from your state insurance commissioner's office. Don't take "no" for an answer until you've run out of options, and that won't be for a long, long time.

▶ **Although you may feel discouraged and in no mood for fighting, it doesn't make economic sense to take "no" for an answer from your insurance company for damage you honestly feel should be covered.**

Following any major disaster, your fellow Americans, elected officials, and the media are paying attention to the way insurance companies treat survivors. That pressure will help you to get a fair shake. Don't give up if it's still very early in the process—or you may undersettle your claim.

Q ▪ *Are there "good" and "bad" insurance companies?*

A ▪ Some insurance companies have the reputation of being more fair and more prompt in handling claims than others, but it's hard to predict what's going to happen in an unprecedented situation. Working together with neighbors, following UP's claim tips, and using the materials in your three-ring binder will really increase your chances of getting treated well and promptly.

Q ▪ *The insurance adjuster tells me my foundation is still good.*

A ▪ Get a second opinion before rebuilding on an existing slab/foundation. Concrete can "fail" due to damage that an untrained eye won't see. Most adjusters have no training in concrete science.

Q ▪ *Labor and material prices have jumped sky high, but the insurance company will pay only according to its "pricing guidelines." The guidelines are inaccurate and really out of date. What can I do?*

A ▪ Labor and material costs always go up after disasters because of supply, demand, and greed. Your insurance company owes you for what it will cost in **real life, not on paper** (up to your policy limits). Guideline pricing is something insurance companies use to predict how much materials and labor should cost. This system is often a problem because reality demands flexibility. No one can accurately predict how much prices will change after a disaster.

Take plywood for example. Its price fluctuates wildly and can vary from $12 per sheet up to $25 per sheet in a post-disaster scenario. That doesn't make it right, but it's not fair or legal to make you wait until things stabilize to start repairing/rebuilding your home.

Roofs are a highly contested item. If the insurance company's pricing is $150 per square foot but the market price is $240 per square foot, keep all receipts and demand the difference along with all the amounts the insurance company "held back" due to actual cash value (ACV) rules. (See UP's Tips for details.)

The National Flood Insurance Program (NFIP) has pricing lists of what they will pay pre-repair. If your pricing increases, you can go back with a supplemental claim, and they should pay the adjusted price.

Q ▪ *There are no houses available to rent in my area. My insurance policy covers my temporary/additional living expenses, but there's no place to live. What can I do?*

A ▪ If you're planning to rebuild/repair and stay in the area and are willing to live in a trailer, negotiate with your insurer to "cash out" your additional living expenses (ALE) coverage limits so that you can buy a trailer or motor home with your ALE policy limits, instead of using the money to pay rent.

Insurers have not been offering this option, but they should be. With a large-scale disaster you're going to need every penny of ALE coverage, and then some, to cover your living expenses while you are out of your home. Negotiating a cash out gives you flexibility and saves you from having to submit more receipts and paperwork to your insurance company.

Q ▪ *My home is very badly damaged, but "A" insurance company refuses to pay anything up front for my contractor's overhead and profit. I don't have the cash to advance this item, and he won't start without it, so I'm stuck.*

A ▪ This is a common problem with some insurance companies, and it's unfair. In some states it's illegal. Overhead and profit ("O & P") is a known expense that all contractors charge, usually at a rate of 10% and 10%. An insurer that holds back O & P until repairs are completed puts the property owner in an impossible financial position. It is wrong for your insurance company to hold back O & P until your home is completely repaired. If you have a flood insurance policy, check the NFIP bulletin for specific items that are covered.

Q ▪ *My insurance company keeps reducing what they're going to pay by "depreciating" items in my claim. What can I do?*

A ▪ Read and follow UP's Claim tips. Depreciation is subjective—not a science. Each adjuster makes his or her own decisions about which items he or she depreciates and by how much. This process means it's up to you to argue for more reasonable numbers. Also, not everything in your home is subject to depreciation. For example, paint, vinyl, and roofing are exposed to the elements, so of course they deteriorate and are subject to depreciation. The underlying materials that held your home together—studs, cement, rebar, framing—are not. Studs can last

200 years, so don't allow your adjuster/insurer to depreciate those items.

Adjusters and insurers rarely volunteer to tell you that if you submit receipts for items you replace, they **must** pay you the difference between what they paid you for the item's actual cash value (ACV) and what it actually cost you (if you have a replacement cost, not a strictly ACV policy).

Q ▪ *My adjuster is rushing me to complete my contents inventory, but I just can't remember everything yet.*

A ▪ It's normal and fine not to remember much after a traumatic loss. Take your time and don't rush. As many as 99% of all disaster victims can't remember even most of what they had—even after months and years after their loss. Use the lists in the **Household Inventory Guide** section of this book to help you.

If you allow yourself to be rushed into a fast settlement, you are definitely going to underestimate what you had, and you will get less than you're entitled to. Don't forget to include taxes, transportation, and shipping costs associated with replaced items.

Q ▪ *My home is only partially damaged, but it will look weird if half the vinyl siding is old and half is new. The insurance company tells me they don't owe me for matching. Is that true?*

A ▪ No. Your insurer owes it to you to restore your property to its pre-loss condition, subject to the dollar limits of your coverage. The appearance of your home after repairs have been made is legally supposed to be "**uniform and consistent.**" If you didn't have two colors of siding on your house before the loss, you don't have to have two colors after the loss. Insurance is supposed to put you back where you were before the loss.

Q ▪ *The contractors' estimates I've received are $20,000 and more above the ones the insurance company got. How can I break the logjam and still hire the contractor I trust?*

A ▪ This is a very, very common problem. If you've submitted all the information that your insurance company needs to pay your claim, written follow-up letters and made phone calls to higher-ups in the company, but nothing's worked, consider "mediation" or "appraisal" to resolve the difference. Mediation is an informal way of resolving problems without going to court. Insurance appraisals are like mini-trials without a jury. Almost every homeowner's policy has an Appraisal section that is supposed to help resolve disputes over repair estimates.

If you and your insurance company are far apart on the amount you're owed for repairs, consider using the appraisal process to settle the dispute. If you decide to use this process, *make sure you get help from experts who don't work for the insurance industry, or you'll be wasting your time and money.*

Email insurance-related questions to:
info@unitedpolicyholders.org.

Chapter 6

Tax Help for Casualty & Disaster Victims

Recovery help from casualty and disaster losses comes from an unexpected source: the Internal Revenue Service. The IRS allows taxpayers who itemize their deductions to deduct casualty losses. The IRS defines a casualty loss as the damage, destruction, or loss of property from an identifiable event that is sudden, unexpected, or unusual. Casualty losses are usually claimed on your income tax filing for the year of the loss. Although all casualty losses will feel like a disaster to the people involved, the tax treatment of a presidentially declared disaster provides greater relief to the victims.

To claim any casualty loss, you have to fill out extra paperwork and keep good records. You also won't recover dollar-for-dollar the financial costs you suffered. However, every little bit helps. For major disasters, it's usually worth the effort to claim the tax deduction.

Having where you live declared a federal disaster can help some property owners obtain much-needed cash a bit more quickly. The wait for tax refund money attributable to disaster losses is cut dramatically when a house, car, or business is damaged or destroyed by an event deemed a major disaster by the president. In these cases, taxpayers can deduct their losses in the tax year before the event happened by filing an amended return.

When the Federal Emergency Management Agency (FEMA) announces that the President has declared a major disaster in certain areas, the way is cleared for special federal help, including tax options.

The process. First, your casualty loss must meet IRS deductibility guidelines. The losses can result from natural or man-made disasters. Examples cited in the IRS literature include:

- Fires
- Burglaries and thefts
- Storms, such as ice storms and blizzards
- Tornadoes
- Floods
- Hurricanes
- Earthquakes
- Vandalism
- Mudslides
- Drought (if sudden in nature)

Natural wear and tear isn't a casualty loss. The IRS won't accept claims for lost property, termite damage to your home, mold damage from a slow water leak, or the death of your prize birch tree to disease.

After you've established that your loss is allowable, you need to figure out exactly how much you can deduct. The IRS sets two limits. First, you must reduce the amount you can claim by $100. Second, you have to reduce the total of all your casualty losses by 10% of your adjusted gross income. The arithmetic is shown in an example later in this chapter.

As a result of a major disaster, such as Hurricane Katrina, Congress may choose to lift the preceding limitations. For instance, in October 2005, a little more than month after the disaster, a new law removed these limits for Hurricane Katrina losses so that the entire amount became deductible. To qualify, a loss must be attributable to Hurricane Katrina, and it must have occurred after August 24, 2005, in the presidentially declared disaster area. The $100 and 10% limits still apply to losses that were not caused by Hurricane Katrina. For 2005, **Form 4684, Casualties & Thefts**, was revised to reflect the new law for Hurricane Katrina losses.

Disaster-related tax relief often includes extended filing deadlines and easing of related penalties for individuals and businesses located in the designated disaster areas. The relief also usually applies to those whose tax records are located in the damaged regions (at an accountant's office, for example), and workers from any location who are there providing help to victims. Workers assisting in the relief activities in the covered disaster areas are eligible for relief whether or not they are affiliated with a recognized government or philanthropic organization. These people should also mark their appropriate forms with the designated name of the qualified disaster such as "Wyoming Tornado," "California Fires," or "Hurricane Katrina" written in red ink at the top of the form.

In addition, taxpayers in federal disaster areas have the option to amend their previous year's tax returns and claim the catastrophic losses they suffered this year on the old return. In many instances, amended filing will make the individual eligible for an immediate tax refund—money that can be used to live on or to begin repairs.

Filing an amended return is often a good idea for taxpayers who didn't itemize deductions the previous year. If the total of the casualty loss and any other itemized deductions amount to more than the standard deduction they originally took, refiling is generally to their advantage. Even taxpayers who did itemize may find an amended return worthwhile if the disaster damage produces more than they originally deducted.

Caution. Although the option to time-shift federal disaster casualty losses to the previous year is a great advantage for some, it's not the best move for all taxpayers. Some disaster victims may find that although their losses are considerable, they aren't enough to meet the two tax-law limits on casualty claims.

Tax experts also say that people who had very high taxable incomes the year in which they could claim the losses and expect very low incomes in the year of the disaster may be able to deduct more of their losses by waiting until they file their returns the following year. Evaluate your individual circumstances—tax, damage, and financial recovery needs—carefully. Be sure that the disaster is a certified federal disaster to get immediate relief.

If you meet the loss limits, the process to claim them is the same regardless of whether you file an amended return or wait until the next filing season. The first step is to gather the proper forms. You need **Form 4684** to figure and report your casualty loss and **Schedule A** to itemize your loss deduction. Attach both of these to your individual income **Form 1040** tax return. If you need to file an amended return to claim losses, use **Form 1040X** instead. You don't have to include supporting documents with your return, but you need those records to help you complete **Form 4684** and to verify your expenses and losses if the IRS ever questions the deduction.

The next step is to determine how the damage has hurt your property's fair market value. This is a two-part valuation—what your property was worth immediately before the catastrophe and what it's worth afterward.

You must figure the value of your "adjusted basis." If you acquired the property as a gift, an inheritance, or in a nontaxable exchange, look at **IRS Publication 551** for an explanation of how to figure your adjusted basis. For homes, this usually is the cost of the property plus adjustments that add to the value, such as improvements to the structure, fencing, or permanent landscaping less previous casualty losses. For vehicles or other personal property, it may be depreciation that reduces its value. Then get an appraisal for the value of the property before and after the disaster. This is how you determine the decrease in the fair market value (FMV) of the property as a result of the casualty or theft.

Disaster victims should also think about damage to the property that is an indirect result of the casualty. Some examples are destroyed doors, windows, shrubbery, and plants.

From the smaller of the adjusted basis or decrease in FMV, subtract any insurance or other reimbursements you received or expect to receive. This figure is the amount of your deductible loss. The purpose of comparing the adjusted basis to the reduction in FMV is to limit your loss to no more than what your cost was in the property.

Impact of insurance. Once the loss is determined, use **Form 4684** to figure the deductible amount of your casualty loss. You must reduce the initial loss claim amount by any insurance or other reimbursement you have received. If you have insurance on your property, you must submit a claim in order to use the damage to it as a casualty loss. In other words, you can't decide you don't want to pay the deductible your insurance would require and then use the total, unreimbursed loss amount as your casualty claim. All claims for damage must first be submitted to the property owner's insurance carrier, *even if the property is not covered*, in order to take a casualty loss deduction. All insurance payments must be used to repair or replace your property, or any excess not used for these purposes may be a taxable gain.

You must be able to show that you actually spent the money for the replacement property for at least the amount of the insurance proceeds. Replacement by gift or inheritance does not qualify.

Like-kind replacement. The IRS allows taxpayers to elect to defer the tax on any gain realized from the casualty if certain conditions are satisfied. The replacement property must be similar to the property that was destroyed. For example, if your *home* is destroyed and you use the insurance proceeds to buy a *mini-market,* this is not like-kind property. To be similar or related in service or use, the replacement property has to be used as your *home.* If your lost building was rental property, then you need to replace it with a rental property to be like-kind. Personal use property must be replaced with similar use personal property. In other words, your household contents are treated as a separate group from your house itself.

Generally, you figure your gain or loss separately for each item, but you treat real estate used for personal purposes, such as your home, as one item (including the land, buildings, trees, and other improvements). If your main home, or any of its contents, is damaged or destroyed as a result of a disaster in a presidentially declared disaster area, do not report any gain due to insurance proceeds you receive for unscheduled personal property (such as damaged furniture) that was part of the contents of your home. This provision alone can provide significant tax relief to major disaster victims.

Any other insurance proceeds received for the home or its contents can be treated as being received for a single item of property. Any replacement property you purchase that is similar or related in service or use to your home or its contents is treated as similar or related in service or use to that single item of property. You can choose to recognize gain only to the extent that the insurance proceeds are more than the adjusted basis of your replacement property. If you choose to postpone any gain from the insurance proceeds you received, the period for purchasing replacement property is 4 years after the close of the first tax year in which any gain is realized. Although it may not be practical from a cash-flow aspect, a tax planning tip for disaster victims is to receive your first payment from the insurance company for contents or buildings after December 31st if your loss occurred toward the end of the year. This would result in a later begin-date for the replacement period.

For renters. Renters qualify for relief under these rules if the rented residence is their main home. The IRS then requires you to reduce your loss by $100. Finally, reduce the total yet again by 10% of your adjusted gross income to get to your final casualty loss deduction.

Worksheet example. Worksheet A on the next page shows the computations for a hypothetical Susan Taxpayer, who suffered through a federally declared flood disaster. The water substantially damaged Susan's home, the property inside her home, and her car. Insurance covered only part of her losses.

Susan's adjusted gross income is $60,000, and that's what she uses to figure her casualty deduction. Susan was taking a break from work—and without pay—for the week that her employer was closed during the flood. Unfortunately, Susan cannot claim the lost income. The IRS provides no deduction for missed wages, even in the event of federal disasters.

Susan, a single filer, decided to amend her 2004 tax return because she took only the standard deduction of $4,750 when she filed that year. The larger itemized deduction amount will lower her tax bill and, depending upon how much she paid in taxes last year, she may be eligible for a nice refund. She must write the name of the designated disaster in red ink on the top of her **1040X**. As soon as the IRS gets her amended return, her new refund will be on its way to her.

However, if Susan is not in dire need of the cash, she should run the numbers using 2005 tax rates. Depending on her situation, she may find it more worthwhile from a tax standpoint to claim her disaster losses on the current year's return.

Susan was able to get such a good tax result from her difficult situation because she kept track of what she spent to clean up and repair her property, the main concerns after a disaster strikes.

Worksheet A	House and Land	Property	Auto	Total
1. Original Property Cost plus improvements, less depreciation and prior casualty losses (basis)	$100,000	$50,000	$18,000	$168,000
2. Fair Market Value before disaster	$150,000	$25,000	$12,000	$187,000
3. Fair Market Value (appraisal) after disaster	$75,000	$5,000	$4,000	$84,000
4. Decrease in value (line 2 minus line 3)	$75,000	$20,000	$8,000	$103,000
5. Smaller of line 1 or line 4	$75,000	$20,000	$8,000	$103,000
6. Insurance reimbursement	$50,000	$5,000	$4,000	$59,000
7. Loss after reimbursement (line 5 minus line 6)	$25,000	$15,000	$4,000	$44,000
8. Total loss (total of line 7 entries):				$44,000
9. Subtract $100 (Use $0 if loss is attributable to Hurricane Katrina in the Presidentially-declared disaster area.				−$100
10. Loss after $100 rule				$43,900
11. Subtract 10% of Adjusted Gross Income (Use $0 if loss is attributable to Hurricane Katrina in the Presidentially-declared disaster area.				−$6,000
12. Amount of casualty loss deduction				$37,900

Your deduction is *not* the amount of your refund. You must refigure your taxes using this new deduction (entered on **Schedule A** and **Form 1040** or **1040X**) to determine just how much you will receive as a refund.

Keep in mind, however, that the tax laws won't allow you to specifically get back that $5,000 you paid to have the carpets cleaned after the flood. There is no place on **Form 4684** for you to enter this expense and have it count directly as part of your casualty loss deduction.

However, because her flooring was damaged by the flood, Susan can use what she spent to repair it as a measure of how much her home's property value was reduced by the storm. This in turn will give her a more accurate assessment of her property's damage and the tax deduction value of the loss she suffered.

In Susan's case, the $75,000 post-disaster value of her home takes the floor damage into account. If the carpets didn't need professional cleaning, then her home might be worth $80,000. This would mean that the amount she could claim as a casualty loss would be only $32,900, and her tax relief would be less.

The IRS points out that expenses for repairs should take care of only the damage. You can't have the repair team improve on the original status of your property.

Record keeping. Even though the IRS allows disaster victims some tax leeway, the agency still demands that casualty losses, like every deduction, be substantiated and supported.

The IRS does not require you to keep your records in a particular way, only that you keep them in a manner that allows you and the IRS to determine your correct tax. Although you don't have to submit your documentation with your return, you should keep your records handy and be able to show the following if asked:

- The type of casualty and when it occurred.
- That the loss amount claimed was a direct result of the casualty.
- That you were the owner of the property or, if you leased it, that you were contractually liable to the owner for the damage.

There are two main ways to track loss substantiation. The simplest way to track it is via your checkbook. There you can enter income and loan or insurance reimbursement deposits, along with all checks written for expenses accrued in connection with your disaster loss. Be specific. Note amounts, sources of deposits, and types of expenses. You may think you will remember them, but it may be years before you are asked about your entries.

If you use a credit card to pay expenses, then keep a spiral notebook to keep track of your charges. Also, **get a *separate* credit card** to pay expenses, along with a spiral notebook to list your charges. Attach your charge slips to your monthly statement to use in case of an IRS audit or to substantiate your insurance costs. **Rewards tip**: By charging building supplies, clothing, appliances, etc. on a credit card that accumulates rewards points, you may be able to earn a large rebate, or you may be able to cash in points for free airline miles if you can get that kind of benefit on your credit card.

Holding on to other documents, such as receipts and sales slips, can also help prove a deduction. Keep your records in an orderly fashion, such as placing documents related to a particular event in a designated envelope and, where applicable, store them by year and type of income or expense.

And don't forget your camera. Photographs showing the original condition of the property and ones taken after the disaster struck can be helpful in establishing the condition and value of your property. If your pre-disaster pictures were destroyed, ask your family to look through their albums for pictures that might help.

When you do send in your amended return, explain that the refiling was due to casualty losses incurred in a federal disaster and attach **Form 4684** to show how you figured your loss. Be sure to specify the date or dates of the disaster and the city, county, and state where the damaged or destroyed property was located when the disaster occurred.

Delayed damages. What if you thought you escaped the disaster but, instead, discover it was just a bit slow in arriving? This might be the case if you live in a federal disaster area and state or local officials decide that your home must be moved or torn down for public safety reasons, such as ensuing mud slides.

You still can take advantage of the casualty loss deduction as long as the government-ordered demolition or relocation of your home is issued within 120 days after the original federal disaster declaration. Your resulting loss is treated just as if it occurred in the natural disaster.

In addition, if your casualty or theft loss causes your deductions to be more than your income for the year you claim the loss, you may have a net operating loss, or NOL. An NOL can be used to lower your tax in an earlier year, allowing you to get a refund for tax you already paid, or it can be used to lower your tax in a future year. You do not have to be in business to have an NOL from a casualty or theft loss. For more information, see **Publication 536, Net Operating Losses (NOLs) for Individuals, Estates, and Trusts**.

Taxable gain. Because insurance payments must be used to repair or replace your property, any excess not used for these purposes may be a taxable gain to you. You can postpone paying tax on some or all of the gain if you buy a replacement property within 2 years *after the close of the first tax year in which any part of your gain is realized* (you received an insurance payment). The replacement period begins when your property was damaged, destroyed, or stolen. Loss of your main home in a presidentially declared disaster area changes the period to 4 years instead of 2. If your main home was damaged or destroyed and you received insurance payments that were more than the adjusted basis, you have a gain. (For more information about how to calculate your adjusted basis, refer to **IRS Publication 551**). You may have a gain even if your property decreased in fair market value (FMV) but if it is smaller than your adjusted basis. Look at the following examples:

Gain from insurance proceeds for ordinary casualty loss (Worksheet B). Assume Tom's house, with an adjusted basis of $100,000, was completely destroyed by a tornado. The contents, with a basis of $40,000, were also destroyed. The insurance company paid Tom $130,000 for the residence and $42,000 for the contents, resulting in a realized gain of $30,000 on the house and $2,000 on the contents. Within 2 years of the event, he spent $132,000 to purchase a new principal residence and $50,000 to replace his personal property. Tom can elect to defer the realized gain. If he does so, the basis of the new residence will be $102,000 ($132,000 purchase price minus $30,000 of deferred gain) and $48,000 in the new personal property ($50,000 minus $2,000 deferred gain). If Tom spent only $120,000 on a new residence and $40,000 on the contents, he would have a taxable gain of $10,000 on the house (the amount of the gain not reinvested in a replacement residence) and $2,000 on the contents.

Gain on insurance proceeds in a presidentially declared disaster (Worksheet C). Assume again that Tom was paid $130,000 for his house and $42,000 for its contents by his insurance company for damages caused by the same tornado that became a presidentially declared disaster. Again, assume his basis in the house was $100,000 and his basis in the property was $40,000. However, $7,000 of the $42,000 contents insurance payment was received for the destruction of scheduled property (such as separately insured jewelry or antiques) with a basis of $4,000 (the balance was "other contents"). The federal disaster designation allows him to treat $142,000 ($130,000 for the

Worksheet B	House and Land	Total Contents
1. Original Property Cost plus improvements, less depreciation and prior casualty losses (basis)	$100,000	$40,000
2. Fair Market Value before disaster	$110,000	$30,000
3. Fair Market Value (appraisal) after disaster	$0	$0
4. Decrease in value (line 2 minus line 3)	$110,000	$30,000
5. Smaller of line 1 or line 4	N/A	N/A
6. Insurance reimbursement	$130,000	$42,000
7. Gain after reimbursement (line 6 minus line 1)	$30,000	$2,000
8. Replacement property acquired	$132,000	$50,000
9. New tax basis for replacement property	$102,000	$48,000
10. Gain recognized	$0	$0

house and $7,000 for the scheduled property) with a basis of $104,000 ($100,000 plus $4,000) as a "common pool" of funds. If he spends at least $137,000 on a replacement residence and similar use scheduled property, he will have no taxable gain. If he spends only $118,000 on both types of property, he will have a taxable gain of $24,000 ($142,000 minus $118,000). The house, land, and scheduled property are treated as one asset.

A replacement home tax tip. If Tom does not use the entire $137,000 to purchase a new primary residence, the gain may not be taxable under the sale of personal residence provisions if he lived in the home for at least 2 years out of the last 5. See **Publication 523, Selling Your Home**, for more details about how to qualify to exclude up to $250,000 of gain ($500,000 for a married couple).

As a warning, however, you need to consider the experience of the Knowles family after a California fire. The insurance company paid $150,000 immediately after the fire for the appraised value of their destroyed home. With the benefit of replacement value insurance, the Knowles family received an additional

Worksheet C	House and Land	Scheduled Property	Total	Other Contents
1. Original Property Cost plus improvements, less depreciation and prior casualty losses (basis)	$100,000	$4,000	$104,000	$36,000
2. Fair Market Value before disaster	$110,000	$7,000	$117,000	$23,000
3. Fair Market Value (appraisal) after disaster	$0	$0	$0	$0
4. Decrease in value (line 2 minus line 3)	$110,000	$7,000	$117,000	$23,000
5. Smaller of line 1 or line 4	N/A	N/A	$0	N/A
6. Insurance reimbursement	$130,000	$7,000	$137,000	$35,000
7. Gain after reimbursement (line 6 minus line 1)	$30,000	$3,000	$33,000	$0
8. Replacement property acquired	$137,000	$0	$137,000	$35,000
9. New tax basis for replacement property	$104,000	$0	$104,000	$35,000
10. Gain recognized	$0	$0	$0	$0

$35,000 for the actual cost of rebuilding. If you receive only the appraised value insurance proceeds, you may be receiving less than you could have for your loss.

If you own a second property, such as a vacation home, and received insurance payments that were more than the adjusted basis for the loss of that property, you may be able to postpone some or all of the gain by buying replacement property—but you must do so within 2 years, not 4.

IRS Pub. 547 provides more information on the required election statement when the replacement property is acquired in a year other than the year in which the gain is realized—i.e., when the insurance proceeds are received.

The 2-year and 4-year replacement deadlines are a concern for major disaster victims, such as those affected by Hurricane Katrina. As expressed by California CPA Robert L. Castle, the estimated timeline to determine whether Katrina's land would be suitable for building upon may take up to 2½ years. (The Army Corps of Engineers estimated that it would take from 60 to 90 days to repair the levees, plus at least a year to remove all of the debris caused by the hurricane. Then it would take another year for the ground to dry out so that land can be evaluated for building suitability.) The Katrina disaster was so large that companies like Boise Cascade, Weyerhaeuser, Georgia Pacific, and Louisiana Pacific—the prime manufacturers of lumber, plywood, and sheet rock used in the construction of houses and buildings—projected that they may not be able to produce enough raw material to get everybody rebuilt in a 4-year time frame. Unless this disaster receives special treatment after this chapter was written, some Katrina victims may be wise to buy a replacement property in order to make the time deadlines.

An example of a precedent for a special extension can be found with **New York Liberty Zone**, which provides an extension for business property from the usual 2-year replacement period for a tax-free replacement of involuntarily converted property to 5 years for Liberty Zone property converted as a result of the September 11, 2001 terrorist attack.

Temporary living expenses. Many homeowners' policies provide some relief for temporary living expenses. If your insurance pays you more than your increase in living costs, you must include the excess as "Other Income" on your tax return. However, if the casualty occured in a presidentially declared disaster area, none of the living expense insurance payments are taxable. A temporary increase in your living expenses is the difference between the actual living expenses you incurred during the time you could not use your home and your normal living expenses for that same period. Actual living expenses are the reasonable and necessary expenses incurred because of the loss of your main home. These expenses include rental of suitable lodging, transportation, food, utilities, rental of furnishings, and other miscellaneous services. If you would normally pay $625 in rent or mortgage payments and $100 for utilities and you have to live instead in a motel for a total of $1,600, your increase in living expenses is $875. If the insurance company payment for living expenses is $1,100, then you have a taxable gain of $225. As long as you are obligated to pay your regular mortgage payments, these payments will be added to the $1,600 motel bill. The $225 in taxable income disappears and you have an itemized deduction to the extent that the payments are applied to mortgage interest.

Assistance payment status. Tax relief assistance payments are not generally taxable. People in a presidentially declared disaster area who receive grants from state programs, charitable organizations, or employers to cover medical, transportation, or temporary housing expenses do not include these grants in their income.

Losses on business or rental property also qualify for tax relief. Different rules apply to figuring this deduction. Small business owners can take advantage of "involuntary conversion rules for disaster damage" that provide further assistance to business owners whose property was damaged, or involuntarily converted, in presidentially declared disasters. Property used in a business that is damaged by a natural disaster is eligible for nonrecognition of gain under the law, which means that qualified replacement property can be purchased and the gain can be deferred, offering tax relief to disaster victims. Essentially, the property is treated as a "trade-in" on the replacement property instead of a "sale" for the amount of insurance proceeds.

This provides relief for businesses that are forced to suspend operations for a substantial time due to the property damage. In other words, if a business loses valuable customers during the business closure and the business fails, the owners may want to consider reinvesting their capital in a new business venture in order to defer tax gain.

If your income-producing property is completely destroyed or stolen, the decrease in fair market value is not a factor. Your loss is the adjusted basis of the property, minus any salvage value and any insurance or other reimbursement you receive or expect to receive.

The IRS will waive the usual fees and expedite requests for copies of previously filed tax returns for people who need them to apply for benefits or to file amended returns claiming disaster-related losses. Write the designated disaster name, such as "Hurricane Katrina," in red ink at the top of **Form 4506, Request for Copy of Tax Return,** or **Form 4506-T, Request for Transcript of Tax Return.**

Selected On-Line Resources.

- Form 4684, Casualties & Thefts:
  http://www.irs.gov/pub/irs-pdf/f4684.pdf
- Schedule A, Itemized Deductions:
  http://www.irs.gov/pub/irs-pdf/f1040sab.pdf
- Form 1040, Individual Income Tax Return:
  http://www.irs.gov/pub/irs-pdf/f1040.pdf
- Form 1040X, Individual Amended Income Tax Return:
  http://www.irs.gov/pub/irs-pdf/f1040x.pdf
- Disaster Losses Kit for Individuals:
  http://www.irs.gov/pub/irs-pdf/p2194.pdf
- Publication 2194B, Disaster Losses Kit for Businesses:
  http://www.irs.gov/pub/irs-pdf/p2194b.pdf
- American Bar Association, Section of Taxation Hurricane
  Katrina Disaster Relief:
  http://www.abanet.org/tax/katrina/affected.html
- IRS publication 551, Basis of Assets: http://www.irs.gov/publications/p551/index.html
- Request for copy of tax return:
  http://www.irs.gov/pub/irs-pdf/f4506.pdf
- Request for transcript of tax return:
  http://www.irs.gov/pub/irs-pdf/f4506t.pdf
- 2005 Federal Disaster Declarations:
  http://www.fema.gov/news/disasters.fema
- Publication 523 (2004), Selling Your Home:
  http://www.irs.gov/publications/p523/index.html
- IRS: Tax Relief in Disaster Situations:
  http://www.irs.gov/newsroom/article/0,,id=108362,00.html
- New Tax Law Eases Loss Limitations for Katrina Victims (Oct
  2005): http://www.irs.gov/newsroom/article/0,,id=149500,00.html
- Net Operating Losses (NOLs) for Individuals, Estates, and
  Trusts: http://www.irs.gov/pub/irs-pdf/p536.pdf
- Selling Your Home: http://www.irs.gov/pub/irs-pdf/p523.pdf

☞ *Use red ink to write the disaster designation
(such as "Hurricane Katrina") on the top of forms
submitted to obtain special treatment, such as
waiver of fees and waiver of penalties.*

For more detailed information about your taxes during
times of disaster, consult your local tax preparer. We recom-

mend consulting with an enrolled agent, a certified public accountant, or a tax attorney because these people are licensed to practice before the Internal Revenue Service. They have passed a rigorous test to demonstrate their tax knowledge and have a high standard of continuing education.

☞ *The Internal Revenue Service (IRS) typically establishes a toll-free telephone number for tax questions following a presidentially declared disaster. The IRS representative should be able to help you get free copies of tax return transcripts, find out about tax relief, and get Disaster Tax Loss Kits. You may also be referred to the Federal Emergency Management Agency's assistance lines for additional help.*

Other taxes. Tax relief includes more than income taxes. Real estate taxes paid by individuals and businesses as well as unsecured property taxes paid by businesses are based on value at a set date each year. A reduction in taxes can be built into the local tax code or can be granted by local taxing authorities after a general or presidentially declared disaster. Relief can be received when the county or city reduces the cost of building permits or waives school fees normally charged on new homes. Be sure to check with local authorities to determine if relief is available and how to make a claim.

Property tax bills are normally mailed at the end of the year, but Hurricanes Katrina and Rita washed away or badly damaged thousands of Louisiana homes. Some Louisiana state lawmakers wanted to postpone the deadline for payment of real estate taxes on those homes. This type of relief to disaster victims creates another problem because it temporarily erases the main source of money that city councils, school boards, and other local governmental units need to provide garbage collection, school buses, and other services.

Before Hurricane Katrina, Louisiana law required a reassessment appraised on a home's value based on its condition the day the flood damage occurred. People whose homes were completely destroyed would pay taxes only on the value of the land. Current state law allowed for such a reassessment only after flood damage and not after wind damage. This law prompted the Louisiana legislature to discuss this difference in disaster treatment. It also proposed a bill under which homeowners with hurricane-damaged homes would pay property taxes at their full assessment level for the months before the storm. The rest of the tax invoice would be based on the lesser tax rate after the storm damage and reassessment. Another bill proposed that homeowners with a homestead exemption on the first $75,000 of its value should be allowed to keep that exemption even if they're not currently living there because of storm damage.

The message to remember is that local, state, and federal governments must collect taxes to provide services to their citizens. However, for local and presidentially declared disasters, elected officials often want to do what they can to help their constituents to recover as quickly as possible from the catastrophe. Even if there is no built-in relief under the law at the time of the disaster, local officials may waive school fees, building permits, personal property taxes, real estate taxes, and local income taxes. Be aware of these changing sources of tax relief.

**If you want to contact Susan Knowles,
you can reach her through her Web site
at www.knowlesoffice.com.**

Chapter 7

Making Lists & Making Sense of These Lists

The lists in the following chapters are taken from *The Household Inventory Guide: Ideas and Lists for Stocking, Restocking, and Taking Stock of Your Home*, which was written as a result of the 1991 Oakland–Berkeley Firestorm. The chapters have been revised and updated, with both additions and deletions.

The lists are intended to help you recall and record your personal property or content losses and also to help you replace what was destroyed. The pages are meant to be marked up and written on.

If you are using the lists for insurance, tax, or legal purposes, you may be looking for specific items. Although the chances are good that whatever you are trying to find (or something similar enough to remind you of it) *is* in here somewhere, it may not be listed exactly where you expect to find it. As you continue through the chapters, however, you should be able to compile a very thorough inventory.

The way the lists and chapters in this book are presented takes into account the various types and sizes of homes that readers have (from studio apartments to houses with multiple bedrooms), and it also reflects the notion that the way we organize our things and where we keep them is probably as unique as our fingerprints.

Keeping these differences in mind, the household inventory chapters are partly organized according to the kinds of rooms and spaces we have in our homes, such as **Kitchen, Bedroom, The Laundry Area**, and so on. These chapters contain lists of things commonly found in these particular rooms or spaces except for appliances, furniture, and furnishings. Because **Appliances, Furniture, & Furnishings** span all the rooms of a home, they merit a chapter of their own and are not usually mentioned elsewhere. That means that under **Kitchen**, for instance, you will not find stove or refrigerator. Instead, you will find dishes, a cookie jar, birthday candles, and soap—common things found on counters and in cupboards and drawers in a kitchen area. Bedding is listed under **Bedroom**, but bed is not.

Other chapters list items that don't fit neatly into any one type of room or space. Examples of these categories include **Books**, **Pet Supplies**, and equipment for **Recreation, Sports, & Exercise**.

Some items are listed in more than one place. For example, you will find aspirin on the medicine shelf in the **Kitchen**, in the **Bathroom**, and in the "First Aid Kit" listed under **Emergency Supplies**. Luggage can be found in both the **Storage** and **Travel** chapters.

We occasionally use brand names. This usage should not be taken as an endorsement for any particular product. Rather, the names are given as examples of a certain kind of item to clarify meaning. For instance, most of us instinctively ask for a Band-Aid when we cut ourselves, regardless of what brand of adhesive strips we use.

As you begin to restock your household, you need to distinguish between what you need right now and what you may want to add later in order to live comfortably. For instance, you may need a bed to sleep in right now. If you want a headboard or a canopy, you can deal with that later. You will need cutlery for food preparation but can make do without a grapefruit knife. You should begin with the absolute basics, and **The Short List** will get you started. The fleshing out will come in time.

Chapter 8

The Short List

This chapter will not help you with insurance losses. Rather, it is a guide to
help you replace what you lost. It may
take a long time before you are able to
shop for anything that is not essential. For
a while, thinking will probably be secondary
to acting or reacting. Still, when you are left with little or nothing with which to begin again, you need to make quick decisions
about what you need first or most in order to get on with the
business of living.

This section is not a list, per se. Rather, it is meant to help
you fashion your own short list according to your individual circumstances. It will act as a guide, taking you through various
chapters and suggesting certain items or categories of things for
you to consider. Page numbers are included for each chapter
mentioned for easy reference.

You may expect the process of making lists to be frustrating,
especially at a time when it is difficult to concentrate and focus
on everything that you need to do. Because the lists in the
household inventory chapters are fairly comprehensive, they
may appear to be cumbersome at first. As you read this chapter,
it will be helpful if you use a bookmark or a paper clip to hold

your place as you skip back and forth between these pages and the other chapters.

We begin with writing materials (i.e., paper or notebooks, pens, pencils, highlighters, etc.) so that you can start writing lists and making notes—both in this book and separately, setting priorities as you go.

If you have not done so already, pick up any prescription drugs, other medications, and first aid supplies that you use on a regular basis or expect to need immediately. You will find ideas for these in the **Bathroom** chapter (pages 106–108) and also in the "First Aid Kit" listed under **Emergency Supplies** (pages 121–124).

Money is a top consideration. Assuming for our purposes here that you have some, the question is, how do you access it? Do you have names of your banks and the numbers of your bank accounts? Do you have an adequate supply of checks? What about credit cards? Do you qualify for emergency assistance? Do you have family, friends, or a group that can provide you with what you need to tide you over?

When you have lost most or all of your belongings, you need clothes, shoes, and personal items to begin with, so turn first to the **Bedroom** chapter (pages 102–105) where the clothes are kept and look through the appropriate lists of clothes. For now, think short term. What kind of shoes, clothes, and accessories will you need in the next few days and weeks? Prioritize. Decide what you must have, taking into account the weather and the kind of clothes you need for work or school, for after work, for weekends, etc.

Think in terms of what you would pack in a suitcase if you were going on a trip. One person who used to travel a lot used to advise people to "Start with your feet, and work your way up and out, so you won't forget anything."

Since you are in the **Bedroom** chapter, you may as well scan the beginning of the list, although we'll come back for bedding later. You may want to add clothes hangers to your list as well as a clock, radio, or clock-radio. Jewelry is not a priority, but if you are without a watch, you may want to replace it now. Even though luggage is on a different list, you should note that you will need suitcases, boxes, bags, or something to put your belongings in. And remember that family, friends, and others will probably be more than happy to provide you with some of these basics.

Continuing to work with the mindset of packing for a trip, go now to the **Bathroom** chapter (pages 106-108) to pick out the personal items you need right away. Think about what you need for just one night away, and begin with the very basics like a toothbrush and toothpaste, a comb, shampoo, razor, etc. Add to these essentials anything else that would make you feel more comfortable or prepared such as a hair dryer, Band-Aids, nail scissors, cologne, and so on.

If you have a baby or young child, go to **Infants & Toddlers** (pages 125-127) or to **Kids' Stuff** (pages 128-129), which is probably where you would begin, even before getting your own clothes and personal items in order. Equipment and supplies for feeding, diapering, and sleeping come to mind first, and what you choose will depend on the age of your child. The **Infants & Toddlers** chapter is comprehensive enough to accommodate little ones of various ages and stages. If you are replacing items from this list, you will want to restock according to your child's current needs.

Because children's clothing is included in the clothes itemized in the **Bedroom** chapter, **Kids' Stuff** primarily covers typical playthings. If your young child has suffered a loss of home, he or she probably needs a few things in this category right away. Stuffed animals, books, and art supplies can be comforting to children and may help open up avenues for them to express feelings. A few toys or games can help keep a restless child occupied while you figure out what to do next.

School children may need to replace backpacks or lunch boxes and, of course, school supplies. A list of the latter can be found in the **Office & School Supplies** chapter (pages 111-113). Similarly, if you have pets, you need to pick up a few things for them immediately. For a list of ideas to get started, look under **Pet Supplies** (pages 130-131).

Many people who are displaced from their homes look for temporary housing while they decide what to do about a more permanent residence. If you are relocating to a furnished home, most of the major appliances and furniture will probably be provided for you. Still, there are a number of items that are not typically included. For instance, in the **Appliances, Furniture, &**

Furnishings chapter (pages 81–85), look under "Appliances" for those items you may need immediately, such as a telephone, lamps, a clock, and a radio. Additional appliances are mentioned in other chapters, notably the **Kitchen**.

If you are moving to an unfurnished home, you need to spend more time reviewing the items listed under "Appliances" and "Furniture." You may also have to decide whether to rent, borrow, or buy used or new furniture, considering how best to meet both your present and future needs. At any rate, to begin you will need furniture to accommodate sleeping, sitting, eating, and storing your things.

Most of the "Furnishings" listed will be low-priority items for now, except for such practical things as waste baskets and a garbage pail, a smoke detector, and maybe a mirror. If you are without window or floor coverings, you may want to include them too.

To begin stocking your household, it is helpful to think in terms of what you think you will use most on an everyday basis for the next couple of weeks. Be selective at first so that your shopping time is well spent, assuming that your shopping time is limited.

Let's start with the **Kitchen** (pages 89–97). You will probably need more items from this list than any other in the beginning. Even so, start with what is absolutely necessary, knowing that you will make many repeat trips to stores as you continue to restock. Let one thing double for another at the outset. A pan can do the job of a teakettle, for example; a mixing bowl can act as a salad or serving bowl; and a paper towel can be used as a coffee filter.

Begin by choosing whatever dishes, silverware, and glasses you will need and continue down the list. You will need some cutlery and maybe a cutting board and assorted cooking utensils. Pick out what you think you will use most for cooking, serving, and storing food. You can probably do without most of the "Electrical Appliances" for now, except perhaps a toaster or coffee maker.

The subsections, "Near the Sink," "Linens," and "Paper Products" have a number of items that you may use on a regular basis, but you can be more selective when you come to "Common Herbs, Spices, & Seasonings." Salt, pepper, and sugar (or their substitutes) are pretty standard in most households. While you're in the spice aisle, however, you might as well add a few of your favorites.

"Cooking & Basic Ingredients & Condiments," "Common Canned & Packaged Cupboard Items," and "Beverages" are subsections loaded with staples. Add to these lists whatever specific "Perishable Goods" you will need as soon as you begin to prepare meals in your home.

The subsection called "The Medicine Shelf" is placed in the **Kitchen**, but other related items are in the **Bathroom** or in the "First Aid Kit" listed in the **Emergency Supplies** chapter.

Next, peruse the subsections "Miscellaneous" and "The Junk Drawer," especially the latter to pick out those things (like scissors, Scotch tape, paper clips, and rubber bands) that we tend to take for granted until we can't find them.

Because many of us have phones in our kitchens, you may need address books and directories along with a calendar and/or an appointment book, borrowed from the **Office & School Supplies** chapter (pages 111–113).

Some linens are mentioned in the **Kitchen** chapter. Now add to those dishtowels, potholders, and so on whatever bedding and towels you will need. The list of bedding is given in the **Bedroom** chapter (pages 102–105). Although sleeping bags are listed elsewhere, you might also include them here if you need them. Return next to the **Bathroom** (pages 106–108) for towels and washcloths. And don't forget toilet paper.

While you are in the **Bathroom** chapter, look toward the end of the list for cleaning supplies and include what you need. More "Cleaning Equipment & Products" are listed in the next chapter, **The Laundry Area** (pages 109–110), where you will find what you need for cleaning and caring for clothes and also for your home and furniture. Again, at first just choose the equipment and products you expect to use within the first week or two. If you need them now, supplies for "Outdoor Garden & Maintenance" are listed at the end of the **Outdoor Living & Maintenance** chapter (pages 114–116).

The **Storage** chapter has an assortment of items that probably deserve to be looked at now. Go to **Storage** (pages 117–120). You may want to pick up some needles and thread, for instance, and a few tools (i.e., hammer, screwdrivers, and measuring tape). You will probably need lightbulbs right away and maybe batteries, string or rope, glue, and an extension cord. Depending on the weather, you might add umbrellas. Also, what about candles, flashlights, shelf-lining material, and maps? Other practical items include clothing hooks, nightlights (and bulbs), and cloth or mesh shopping bags.

You have just completed a guided tour through various chapters and subsections of the *Household Inventory Guide* chapters of this book. I believe we have covered the high priority items and categories for most people. However, you will do well to scan the chapters we skipped if they are important to you. If you are starting over from scratch, you will need list upon list. This section is intended merely as a place to begin.

Chapter 9

Appliances, Furniture, & Furnishings

Appliances, Furniture, & Furnishings is a logical place to begin a book of lists on household goods because most of the big-ticket items in a home are in this category. Knowing what they are in the beginning will help provide an overview of both the placement of these items in your home and the budgeting you may need to do when considering them. If you have to report losses of these items, the lists here will help to jog your memory, although you will have to provide the specifics.

Also, the inventories provided in the following chapters on rooms are oriented more to fleshing out each room or space. These areas will appear bare without the items on this list. The **Bedroom** chapter doesn't list a bed, for instance. The **Dining Room** chapter doesn't list a table, and the **Living and/or Family Room** chapter doesn't list a sofa.

Although you may normally keep lamps, clocks, and waste-baskets in nearly all of the rooms in your home, none of these items are listed in the room chapters. You can choose what you need from this list as you consider the various spaces in your home and add the items to the appropriate lists according to your own needs.

You will notice that most of the furniture is listed as a single item. You may need more than one bookcase or sofa or desk. The list simply supplies the names of furniture commonly found in homes, and you must specify the number of pieces that you need. Also, the names of certain items may be interchangeable, such as bureau, dresser, and chest or coffee/cocktail table.

The list of appliances includes both major appliances and some of the smaller ones as well. Others are listed throughout the various chapters. Toaster is in the **Kitchen**, for example, and hair dryer is in the **Bathroom**. "The Entertainment Center" in the **Living and/or Family Room** chapter gives more detailed information on the television, VCR, and stereo system. The same is true for computers in the **Electronics/Technology** section.

Appliances

- ☐ Refrigerator
- ☐ Freezer
- ☐ Oven & Range
- ☐ Microwave Oven
- ☐ Dishwasher
- ☐ Disposal
- ☐ Washer
- ☐ Dryer
- ☐ Television
- ☐ VCR
- ☐ Stereo System and/or CD Player & Speakers
- ☐ Telephones
- ☐ Answering Machine
- ☐ Computer System
- ☐ Word Processor
- ☐ Lamps & Lighting Fixtures
- ☐ Clocks
- ☐ Radios
- ☐ Clock Radios
- ☐ Air Conditioner (Window/Portable)
- ☐ Ceiling Fan
- ☐ Portable Fan
- ☐ Portable Heater
- ☐ Portable Sewing Machine
- ☐ Alarm System

Furniture

- ☐ Bed (Frame, Box Springs, & Mattress)
- ☐ Headboard and/or Footboard
- ☐ Canopy
- ☐ Rollaway Bed
- ☐ Futon
- ☐ Sofabed
- ☐ Sofa
- ☐ Sectional
- ☐ Loveseat
- ☐ Bench

Chairs

- ☐ Dining room
- ☐ Kitchen
- ☐ Bar Stools
- ☐ Leisure

☐ Lounge

☐ Parlor

☐ Wing

☐ Desk

☐ Office

☐ Folding

☐ Beanbag

☐ Stepladder

☐ Rocker

☐ Recliner

☐ Director's

☐ Lawn

☐ Vanity Stool

☐ Ottoman/Foot Stool

☐ Hassock

Tables

☐ Dining

☐ Kitchen

☐ Coffee/Cocktail

☐ End

☐ Occasional

☐ Lamp

☐ Bedside

☐ Sofa

☐ Parson's

☐ Plant

☐ Mail

☐ Sofa Back

☐ Folding

☐ TV Tray Tables

☐ Card

☐ Drafting

☐ TV Stand

☐ Butcher's Block

☐ Tea Cart

☐ Work Bench

☐ Desk

☐ Bureau

☐ Dresser

☐ Chest

☐ Toy Chest

☐ Cabinet

☐ China Cabinet

☐ Buffet

☐ Hutch

☐ Breakfront

☐ Armoire

☐ Wardrobe

☐ Storage Trunk

☐ Hope Chest/Cedar Chest

☐ Entertainment Center

☐ Large Musical Instruments (i.e., Piano, Organ, Drum Set)

☐ Bookcase

☐ Wall Unit

☐ Shelf Unit

☐ Bathroom Storage Unit

☐ Kitchen Storage Unit

☐ Wine Rack

☐ File Cabinet

☐ Office/Computer Group (i.e., Desk, Hutch, Printer Stand, Corner Connector)

☐ Sewing Machine with Cabinet

☐ Room Divider

☐ Fireplace Screen

☐ Aquarium

Furnishings

Floor Coverings
- [ ] Carpets
- [ ] Rugs
- [ ] Pads

Window Coverings
- [ ] Draperies
- [ ] Curtains
- [ ] Shades
- [ ] Blinds
- [ ] Shutters
- [ ] Valences

Things That Hang on Walls
- [ ] Fine Art
- [ ] Mirrors
- [ ] Tapestry
- [ ] Wallhangings
- [ ] Paintings
- [ ] Framed Pictures,
- [ ] Photographs, Handwork, Diplomas, etc.
- [ ] Plates & Platters with Hanging Plate Holders
- [ ] Posters
- [ ] Plaques
- [ ] Shadow Box with Collection
- [ ] Display Racks
- [ ] Barometer
- [ ] Sconces
- [ ] Clocks
- [ ] Lighting Fixtures
- [ ] Wreath
- [ ] Bulletin Board & Pushpins
- [ ] Chalk Board & Chalk
- [ ] Halltree/Coat Rack
- [ ] Umbrella Stand
- [ ] Chandelier
- [ ] Chimes
- [ ] Decorator Pillows
- [ ] Throws
- [ ] Video Cassette Holders & Cassettes
- [ ] DVD Holder & DVDs
- [ ] CD Holder & CDs
- [ ] Book Ends
- [ ] Antiques & Collectibles
- [ ] Sculpture
- [ ] Figurines
- [ ] Statues
- [ ] Music Box
- [ ] Framed Photographs
- [ ] Plates and Platters
- [ ] Plate Display Stands
- [ ] Planters
- [ ] Plants (Live and/or Artificial)
- [ ] Vases
- [ ] Baskets
- [ ] Bowls
- [ ] Pots
- [ ] Boxes
- [ ] Candlesticks
- [ ] Oil Lamp
- [ ] Decanters
- [ ] Ash Trays
- [ ] Doilies
- [ ] Artificial Fruit

☐ Paper Weight
☐ World Globe
☐ Wastepaper Baskets
☐ Garbage Pail
☐ Recycling Receptacles
☐ Fire Extinguisher
☐ Stepping Stool
☐ Ladder
☐ Holiday & Seasonal Decorations (i.e., Christmas Tree Stand, Skirt, Lights, & Tree & Table Ornaments;

Menorah, Dradle; Decorations for Fourth of July, Halloween, Thanksgiving, etc.)
☐ Religious Items (i.e., Cross, Seder Plate, Scrolls)
☐ Smoke Detectors Protector Pads (Felt or Cork)
☐ Potpourri & Accessories (i.e., Decorative, Simmering, Crystals, Oil, Pot)
☐ Shower Curtain

Chapter 10

Electronics/Technology

Not long ago, many of the items below didn't exist. The lists here are as complete as possible, with the understanding that rapid advances in technology preclude the possibility of ever making a comprehensive list.

Computer Components

- ☐ CPU
- ☐ CD Drive
- ☐ DVD Drive
- ☐ Floppy Drive
- ☐ Keyboard
- ☐ Midi Drives
- ☐ Modem
- ☐ Monitor/s
- ☐ Mouse/Trackball
- ☐ Music Keyboard
- ☐ PC Memory
- ☐ Printer/s
- ☐ Scanner
- ☐ Security Camera
- ☐ Software Programs
- ☐ Sound, Video, & Upgrade Cards
- ☐ Speakers
- ☐ Surge Protector
- ☐ Switches
- ☐ Tape Drive
- ☐ USB Flash Drive/Reader
- ☐ Uninterrupted Power Supply (UPS)
- ☐ Web Camera
- ☐ Zip Drive

Computer Accessories

- ☐ Back & Foot Rests
- ☐ Cables, Connectors, & Switches
- ☐ Cleaning & Maintenance
- ☐ Copyholders

- ☐ Headset
- ☐ Keyboard Drawers
- ☐ Machine Stands
- ☐ Media Labels
- ☐ Mouse Pads & Wrist Rests
- ☐ Notebook Accessories (i.e., Dock)
- ☐ Power Distributor
- ☐ Screen Filters/Protector
- ☐ Speakers & Headset
- ☐ Storage (i.e., Boxes, Racks)
- ☐ USB Flash Memory

Computer Media

- ☐ CD-R/RW
- ☐ Computer Paper (i.e., White, Color, Special Forms)
- ☐ DVD
- ☐ Floppy Diskettes
- ☐ Media Labels
- ☐ Presentation & Meeting Tools
- ☐ Tape Backup & Data Cartridges
- ☐ USB Flash Drive
- ☐ Zip

Handhelds & PDAs with Software & Accessories

- ☐ Cables
- ☐ Docking Cradle
- ☐ Headphones
- ☐ Keyboard for touch-typing
- ☐ LCD Screen Protective Overlay

- ☐ Memory
- ☐ Microphone
- ☐ Modem
- ☐ MP3 & Portable CD Player
- ☐ Protective Cases
- ☐ Rechargeable Batteries
- ☐ Reminder Alarm
- ☐ Screen Care Kit
- ☐ Stylus
- ☐ Travel Portfolio

Copiers & FAX Machines

- ☐ All-in-one Machine
- ☐ Copier
- ☐ Fax Machine
- ☐ Ink & Toner Finder

TV, Home Theater Systems, & Audio Accessories

- ☐ Cinema System
- ☐ Direct TV & Digital Cable TV
- ☐ DVD Player & Recorder
- ☐ DVDs
- ☐ Headphones
- ☐ Home Theater Projector
- ☐ Remote Controls
- ☐ Speaker Stands
- ☐ Televisions & HDTVs
- ☐ TiVo DVRs
- ☐ Video Player & Recorder
- ☐ Video Tapes (Blanks & Movies)

Home Audio & Speakers

- ☐ Amplifier
- ☐ Audio Adaptors & Cables
- ☐ CDs
- ☐ Receiver
- ☐ Records
- ☐ Remote Control
- ☐ Speakers
- ☐ Speaker Cables
- ☐ Subwoofer Cables
- ☐ Tape Cassettes
- ☐ Tuner
- ☐ Turntable

Video Games & Accessories

- ☐ Hardware/Platforms (i.e., PlayStation, Xbox, GameCube)
- ☐ Games (i.e., Play Station 2 Games, Nintendo DS Games, PC Games, Electronic Games)
- ☐ Batteries
- ☐ Cables & Connectors
- ☐ Cases & Organizers
- ☐ Controllers
- ☐ Headphones
- ☐ Memory
- ☐ Strategy Guides

Home Security & Safety

- ☐ Home Security System
- ☐ Security Cameras

Toys & Kids' Electronics

- ☐ Board Games & Puzzles
- ☐ Books
- ☐ Building Sets
- ☐ Dolls, Vehicles, & Playsets
- ☐ Educational Systems & Books
- ☐ Electronic Games
- ☐ Electronic Toys
- ☐ Kids software
- ☐ Musical Instruments & Karaoke
- ☐ Radio-Controlled Vehicles
- ☐ Recreational Toys
- ☐ Riding Toys

Miscellaneous Electronics

- ☐ Binoculars
- ☐ Boombox
- ☐ Calculator
- ☐ Camcorder
- ☐ Cell Phone
- ☐ Cordless Phone
- ☐ Digital Camera & Accessories
- ☐ GPS
- ☐ Home Security & Safety
- ☐ Intercom System
- ☐ Pager
- ☐ Portable Music
- ☐ Radios, Electric & Portable
- ☐ Shredder
- ☐ Speakerphones
- ☐ Telescope
- ☐ Two-way Radio

Chapter 11

Kitchen

The lists here are fairly self-explanatory, except that the locations of some items are arbitrary. Some items are placed in a particular category when they could just as well be placed in another subsection. For example, dishcloths and dishtowels are listed under "Linens" instead of "Near the Sink,"  although they may belong in both places. Coffee filters are in the subsection "Cooking & Storage Equipment & Aids" rather than on the "Paper Products" list because some filters are made of cloth, not paper.

Most of us have what I call "The Junk Drawer," a catch-all space where we keep small, miscellaneous things handy. It may be a shoebox in a cupboard instead of a drawer, and it may be in a different room entirely. But it is listed here because the kitchen is often a central, catch-all kind of place.

Tableware

Set of Dishes
- ☐ Dinner Plates
- ☐ Salad Plates
- ☐ Dessert Plates
- ☐ Bread & Butter Plates
- ☐ Bowls (Cereal/Soup)
- ☐ Cups & Saucers
- ☐ Coffee Mugs
- ☐ Misc. Bowls (i.e., Fruit Compotes)
- ☐ Covered Butter Dish

Flatware

- ☐ Place Knives
- ☐ Butter Knives
- ☐ Steak Knives
- ☐ Place Forks
- ☐ Salad Forks
- ☐ Teaspoons
- ☐ Tablespoons
- ☐ Grapefruit Spoons
- ☐ Misc. &/or Serving Pieces
☐ Divided Flatware Organizer

Glassware

- ☐ Beverage Glasses, Various Sizes
- ☐ Wine Glasses
- ☐ Specialty Glasses

Cooking Utensils

Cutlery

- ☐ Assorted Cutting Knives (i.e., Peeling, Paring, Vegetable, Serrated, Utility, Sandwich, Filet, Boning, Carving, Slicing, French Cook's, Cleaver, Bread)
☐ Knife Rack
☐ Knife Sharpener (Butcher's Steel or Whetstone)
☐ Knife Covers
☐ Cutting Board
☐ Can Opener
☐ Bottle Opener
☐ Wine Opener (i.e., Corkscrew, Cork Puller)
☐ Jar Opener

- ☐ Stirring Spoons
- ☐ Slotted Spoon
- ☐ Ladle
- ☐ Spoon Rest
- ☐ Spatulas, Assorted
- ☐ Potato Peeler
- ☐ Grater
- ☐ Cheese Slicer
- ☐ Rubber Scraper
- ☐ Whisk
- ☐ Tongs
- ☐ Two-Pronged Cook's Fork
- ☐ Pasta Server
- ☐ Measuring Spoons
- ☐ Measuring Cups (Nest for Dry Measure, Glass or Plastic, Assorted Sizes)
- ☐ Colander
- ☐ Strainers
- ☐ Steamer Inset
- ☐ Egg/Rotary Beater
- ☐ Potato Masher
- ☐ Funnels (1 Wide-mouthed)
- ☐ Garlic Press
- ☐ Mallet and/or Meat Pounder
- ☐ Chopping Bowl & Chopper
- ☐ Mortar & Pestle
- ☐ Flour Scoop
- ☐ Flour Sifter
- ☐ Cookie Cutters
- ☐ Cookie Gun
- ☐ Pastry Blender
- ☐ Rolling Pin
- ☐ Rolling Pin Cover & Cloth
- ☐ Pastry Crimper & Sealer

☐ Pastry Decorating Set
☐ Icing Spatula
☐ Utility Scissors
☐ Basting Brush
☐ Baster
☐ Skimmer
☐ Juicer
☐ Citrus Peeler
☐ Apple Corer
☐ Lemon Zester
☐ Grapefruit Knife
☐ Nutcracker & Picks
☐ Fish Scaler
☐ Pizza Wheel
☐ Skewers
☐ Poultry Lacers
☐ Trussing Needles
☐ Butcher's Twine
☐ Turkey Pins
☐ Cheesecloth
☐ Jigger
☐ Bar Shaker

Serving Pieces

☐ Carving Set
☐ Cheese Spreader
☐ Demitasse Spoons
☐ Gravy Ladle
☐ Ice Cream Scoop
☐ Large Spoons (1 Slotted)
☐ Cake Knife
☐ Pie Server
☐ Salad Servers
☐ Two-tined Fork (To reach bottom of jars)

Cooking & Storage Equipment & Aids

☐ Food Scale
☐ Timer
☐ Egg Timer
☐ Bottle Stoppers
☐ Hot Pads and/or Trivets
☐ Oven Thermometer
☐ Refrigerator Thermometer
☐ Meat Thermometer
☐ Candy Thermometer
☐ Tea Diffuser
☐ Coffee Filters
☐ Toothpicks
☐ Matches
☐ Butter Dish
☐ Salt & Pepper Shakers
☐ Pepper Mill
☐ Creamer & Sugar Bowl
☐ Pitchers, Small (Syrup, Gravy, etc.)
☐ Pitchers and/or Jugs, Large (Beverage)
☐ Carafe
☐ Thermos
☐ Insulated Cold/Hot Drink Containers
☐ Mixing Bowls (Nest)
☐ Bread Box/Bin
☐ Storage Containers, Assorted Sizes & Shapes (i.e., Flour, Sugar, Pasta, Coffee, Tea, Crackers, Cookies, Dried Fruit, Leftovers, Misc.)
☐ Wine Rack
☐ Canning Jars

☐ Storage Jars
☐ Cookie Jar
☐ Pie Plate Cover
☐ Covered Cake Plate
☐ Casserole Dishes, Assorted Sizes (Some covered)
☐ Soufflé Molds & Ramekins
☐ Baking Pans, Assorted Sizes & Shapes & Depths
☐ Cookie Sheets
☐ Pie Sheet
☐ Serving Bowls, Assorted Sizes (Some covered)
☐ Salad Bowls
☐ Gravy Boat
☐ Platters
☐ Large Meat/Poultry Platter for Carving
☐ Assorted Hors 'Oeuvres Serving Pieces for Chips & Dip, Crackers & Cheese, Condiments, etc. (i.e., Plates, Trays, Bowls, Platters, Baskets)
☐ Serving Tray (For breakfast in bed or sick tray)
☐ Bread Trays & Baskets
☐ Ice Bucket & Tongs
☐ Fruit Bowl or Basket
☐ Heat Diffuser
☐ Frying/Sauté Pans, Assorted Sizes (Some covered), Wok or Stir-fry Pan
☐ Griddle
☐ Sauce Pans with Lids, Assorted Sizes

☐ Dutch Oven
☐ Stockpot
☐ Broiling Pans
☐ Roasting Pan & Rack
☐ Vertical Poultry Rack
☐ Double Boiler
☐ Pressure Cooker
☐ Omelet Pan
☐ Pizza Pan
☐ Loaf Pans
☐ Pie Plates
☐ Muffin Tins
☐ Cooling Racks
☐ Teakettle
☐ Teapot
☐ Microwave-safe Cookware
☐ Fondue Set
☐ Gelatin/Aspic Molds
☐ Candy Molds
☐ Spice Rack
☐ Recipe Box & Cards
☐ Recipe Card Rack
☐ Cook Books
☐ Ice Trays
☐ Egg Coddlers
☐ Lazy Susan

Electrical Appliances
☐ Blender
☐ Coffee Maker
☐ Crockpot
☐ Food Processor
☐ Mixer (Hand-held and/or Stand)

- [ ] Micro-processor
- [ ] Microwave
- [ ] Rotisserie
- [ ] Grill/Griddle
- [ ] Skillet and/or Wok
- [ ] Toaster
- [ ] Toaster Oven
- [ ] Waffle Iron
- [ ] Can Opener

Gourmet or Specialty Items

- [ ] Coffee Grinder
- [ ] Specialty Coffee Maker (i.e., Espresso, Cappuccino)
- [ ] Pasta Maker
- [ ] Grain Mill
- [ ] Bread Machine
- [ ] Ice Crusher
- [ ] Sandwich Maker
- [ ] Popcorn Popper
- [ ] Ice Cream/Frozen Dessert Maker
- [ ] Yogurt Maker
- [ ] Deep Fat Fryer with Basket
- [ ] Tiered Steamer
- [ ] Fish Poacher with Rack
- [ ] Fondue Set with Fuel
- [ ] Rice Cooker
- [ ] Pizza Stone/Brick
- [ ] Tortilla Maker
- [ ] Portable Barbecue Pit Smoker
- [ ] Food & Meat Chopper or Grinder
- [ ] Meat Slicer

- [ ] Mouli Julienne
- [ ] Citrus Juicer
- [ ] Soda Siphon
- [ ] Salad Spinner

Near the Sink

- [ ] Garbage Pail
- [ ] Soap Dish & Soap Bar
- [ ] Liquid Soap Dispenser & Liquid Soap
- [ ] Sponges
- [ ] Dishpan
- [ ] Sink Mat
- [ ] Dish Drainer/Drying Rack
- [ ] Dishwashing Detergent
- [ ] Dishwasher Detergent
- [ ] Jet Dry
- [ ] Scouring & Abrasive Nylon Pads
- [ ] Cleaning Brushes
- [ ] Vegetable Brush
- [ ] Cleanser
- [ ] Ammonia
- [ ] Silver Polish
- [ ] Sink Stopper
- [ ] Faucet Aerator
- [ ] Swivel Spray Aerator
- [ ] Hand Lotion

Linens

- [ ] Potholders & Oven Mitts
- [ ] Dish Cloths
- [ ] Dish Towels (Tea Towels & Terry Towels)
- [ ] Cloth Napkins & Napkin Rings

☐ Tablecloths
☐ Placemats
☐ Aprons

Paper Products

☐ Paper Towels
☐ Napkins
☐ Cups (Cold Beverage, Hot Beverage)
☐ Shelf-lining Paper
☐ Plates
☐ Lunch Bags
☐ Food Wrap
☐ Foil Wrap
☐ Waxed Paper
☐ Kitchen Parchment (Non-stick Pan-liner)
☐ Sandwich Bags
☐ Food Storage Bags
☐ Freezer Bags
☐ Baking Cups

Common Herbs, Spices, & Seasonings

☐ Allspice
☐ Basil
☐ Bay Leaves
☐ Beau Monde
☐ Beef Bouillon Cubes
☐ Cayenne Pepper
☐ Celery Seed or Salt
☐ Chicken Bouillon Cubes
☐ Chicken Seasoned Stock Base
☐ Chili Powder
☐ Chives

☐ Cinnamon
☐ Cloves (Whole & Powdered)
☐ Cream of Tartar
☐ Cumin
☐ Curry Powder
☐ Dill
☐ Food Coloring
☐ Garlic Powder or Salt
☐ Ginger
☐ Italian Seasoning
☐ Maple Flavoring
☐ Marjoram
☐ Mustard Powder
☐ Nutmeg
☐ Onion Salt, Powder, or Flakes
☐ Oregano
☐ Paprika
☐ Parsley Flakes
☐ Pepper
☐ Peppercorns
☐ Poultry Seasoning
☐ Rosemary
☐ Sage
☐ Salt
☐ Salt Substitute
☐ Seasoning Salt
☐ Sugar Substitute
☐ Sugar, Brown
☐ Sugar, Granulated
☐ Sugar, Powdered
☐ Tarragon
☐ Thyme
☐ Vanilla Flavoring

Cooking & Baking Ingredients & Condiments

- [ ] Oil (i.e., Vegetable, Olive)
- [ ] Vinegar (i.e., Apple Cider, White, Red Wine)
- [ ] Soy Sauce
- [ ] Worcestershire Sauce
- [ ] Teriyaki Sauce
- [ ] Barbecue Sauce
- [ ] Taco Sauce
- [ ] Catsup
- [ ] Mustard, Various Kinds
- [ ] Mayonnaise
- [ ] Pickles (Dill, Sweet)
- [ ] Pickle Relish
- [ ] Tabasco Sauce
- [ ] Horseradish
- [ ] Tartar Sauce
- [ ] Packaged Sauces & Mixes
- [ ] Peanut Butter
- [ ] Jam/Jelly
- [ ] Honey
- [ ] Molasses
- [ ] Maple Syrup
- [ ] Flour
- [ ] Wheat Germ
- [ ] Baking Soda
- [ ] Baking Powder
- [ ] Shortening
- [ ] Cooking Spray
- [ ] Corn Syrup
- [ ] Baking/Pancake Mix
- [ ] Corn Meal
- [ ] Cocoa
- [ ] Gelatin
- [ ] Tapioca
- [ ] Salad Dressing
- [ ] Salsa
- [ ] Olives
- [ ] Pimentos
- [ ] Water Chestnuts
- [ ] Chutney
- [ ] Capers
- [ ] Nuts (i.e., Walnuts, Almonds)
- [ ] Chocolate Chips

Common Canned & Packaged Cupboard Items

- [ ] Soups
- [ ] Beans, Assorted Dry & Canned (i.e., Kidney, Baked, Refried)
- [ ] Tomato Sauce
- [ ] Tomato Paste
- [ ] Pasta Sauce
- [ ] Peeled Tomatoes
- [ ] Meat & Fish (i.e., Deviled Ham, Tuna, Shrimp, Clams)
- [ ] Vegetables
- [ ] Fruit
- [ ] Evaporated Milk
- [ ] Condensed Milk
- [ ] Soy or Rice Milk
- [ ] Powdered Milk
- [ ] Non-Dairy Creamer
- [ ] Cereal
- [ ] Hot Cereal
- [ ] Pasta

☐ Rice

☐ Snack Foods (i.e., Popcorn, Nuts, Crackers, Cookies, Raisins & Other Dried Fruits)

Beverages

☐ Juices

☐ Soft Drinks & Mixers

☐ Bottled Water

☐ Coffee

☐ Tea

Alcoholic

☐ Beer

☐ Wine

☐ Hard Liquor (i.e., Bourbon, Scotch, Gin, Vodka, Brandy)

Perishable Goods

☐ Fresh Fruit

☐ Fresh Vegetables

☐ Bread & Other Bakery Products

☐ Dairy Products

☐ Meat, Fish & Poultry

☐ Frozen Foods & Beverages

The Medicine Shelf

☐ Vitamins & Minerals

☐ Oral Prescription Medications

☐ Aspirin and/or Aspirin Substitutes

☐ Antacid

☐ Cough Medicine

☐ Cough Drops

☐ Cold and/or Allergy Medication

☐ Measuring Vial

☐ Pill Containers

Miscellaneous

☐ Bottled Water (Delivered)

☐ Paper Plate Holders

☐ Paper Towel Holder

☐ Bag Clips

☐ Space Organizers (i.e., Turntables, Storage Baskets, Cup Hooks, China Rack)

☐ Space Savers (i.e., Bi-level Turntables, Expandable Trays with Collapsible Legs)

☐ Refrigerator Magnets

☐ Empty Coffee Cans, Jars, Margarine Tubs for Extra Storage Containers

☐ Grease Can

☐ Straws

☐ Birthday Candles

☐ Toothpicks (Plain for Baking & Fancy for Hors' Oeuvres)

☐ Calendar

☐ Air Freshener

☐ Insulated Lunch Bag/Cooler

☐ Picnic Basket

☐ Cloth or Mesh Shopping Bags

The Junk Drawer

☐ Scissors

☐ Scratch Paper

☐ Pens

☐ Pencils

- ☐ Colored Marking Pens and/or Pencils
- ☐ Scotch Tape
- ☐ Masking/Freezer Tape
- ☐ Paper Clips
- ☐ Ruler
- ☐ Measuring Tape
- ☐ Rubber Bands
- ☐ Post-It Notes
- ☐ Thumb Tacks
- ☐ String

- ☐ A Few Tools (i.e., Screwdrivers, Hammer, Pliers)
- ☐ Envelopes
- ☐ Stamps
- ☐ Return Address Labels or Stamp & Pad
- ☐ Flashlight
- ☐ Matches
- ☐ Spare Keys
- ☐ Gum
- ☐ Candy
- ☐ Wine Corks

Chapter 12

Dining Room

Not everyone has a formal dining room, but even those who don't have a separate room in their home for eating meals may have some of the items listed here. They include many of the more formal things that are nice to have for special occasions, holiday gatherings, or for entertaining guests. Other items on these lists may be similar to or the same as some items in the **Kitchen** chapter.

Dining Room

- ☐ Table Pads
- ☐ Table Cloths and/or Runners
- ☐ Placemats
- ☐ Napkins
- ☐ Napkin Rings
- ☐ Trivets
- ☐ Hot Pads
- ☐ Centerpiece(s)
- ☐ Candlesticks

Set of "Good" Dishes

- ☐ Dinner Plates
- ☐ Salad Plates
- ☐ Bread & Butter Plates
- ☐ Soup Bowls
- ☐ Dessert Bowls & Plates
- ☐ Cups & Saucers
- ☐ Miscellaneous and/or Demitasse Cups Plates & Saucers

Silverware

- ☐ Dinner or Place Knives
- ☐ Butter Knives
- ☐ Dinner or Place Forks
- ☐ Salad Forks
- ☐ Teaspoons
- ☐ Tablespoons
- ☐ Miscellaneous Serving Pieces (Department or jewelry stores with a bridal registry have very complete lists of these pieces.)
- ☐ Silverware Storage Chest

Glassware & Stemware

- ☐ Goblets
- ☐ Wine Glasses
- ☐ Champagne Glasses and/or Flutes
- ☐ Bar Glasses, Assorted Sizes & Shapes (Highball, Martini, Snifter, Cordial, etc.)
- ☐ Punchbowl, Cups & Ladle
- ☐ Pitcher(s)

Tea Service

- ☐ Tray
- ☐ Coffee Server
- ☐ Tea Server
- ☐ Creamer
- ☐ Sugar Bowl & Tongs
- ☐ Slop Bowl
- ☐ Salt & Pepper Shakers
- ☐ Cruet Set
- ☐ Food Warmer
- ☐ Serving Bowls (Some Covered)
- ☐ Serving Plates & Platters
- ☐ Well & Tree Platter
- ☐ Condiment Dishes & Bowls
- ☐ Relish Tray
- ☐ Bread Tray
- ☐ Gravy Boat & Ladle
- ☐ Plate Organizer
- ☐ Wine Cooler and/or Bottle

Chapter 13

Living and/or Family Room

These rooms have been combined because the two rooms tend to serve similar purposes. People use these rooms primarily to relax, to entertain, or to be entertained. We often associate them with listening to music, watching television, reading, and playing games.

Much of what is normally found in a living room or a family room appears in the **Appliances, Furniture, & Furnishings** section where you will find things like sofas, tables, chairs, lamps, and so on. The items on this list flesh out these rooms rather than furnish them.

Living and/or Family Room

Entertainment Center

☐ Television
☐ VCR/DVD
☐ Stereo System
☐ AM/FM Tuner
☐ Cassette Player
☐ Compact Disc Player
☐ Turntable
☐ Reel-to-Reel Tape Player
☐ Speakers
☐ Video Game Player
☐ Video Cassettes & Rack
☐ DVDs & Rack
☐ Cassette Tapes & Rack

☐ Compact Discs & Rack
☐ Records & Rack
☐ Video Games & Rack
☐ TV Stand
☐ Demagnetizer
☐ Record Cleaning Fluid & Applicator
☐ Cassette Tape Cleaner
☐ Portable Cassette Player
☐ Portable Tape Recorder
☐ Portable Radio
☐ Headphones
☐ Walkman
☐ Board & Other Games (i.e., Monopoly, Tripoli, Scrabble, Checkers, Chess, Dominoes, Cribbage, Aggravation, Backgammon, Dungeons & Dragons, Yahtzee, Trivial Pursuit, Pictionary, etc.)
☐ Game Parts (i.e., Poker Chips, Dice, Marbles)
☐ Instruction Books and/or Booklets on Card & Board Games

☐ Playing Cards
☐ Score Cards & Sheets
☐ Bridge Tallies & Score Pads
☐ Paper
☐ Pencils
☐ Drink Coasters
☐ Cocktail Napkins
☐ Coffee Table Book

Fireplace
☐ Screen
☐ Grate or Andirons
☐ Fire Tools
☐ Poker
☐ Tongs
☐ Shovel
☐ Brush
☐ Bellows
☐ Matches & Container
☐ Long Matches
☐ Wood Holder
☐ Magazine Rack
☐ Newspaper Holder

Chapter 14

Bedroom

(Including Clothes)

Like the lists for other rooms, the list for the bedroom does not include the things we probably associate most with this particular room. That's because many of the items commonly found in a bedroom, like bed, dresser, lamps, and so on are listed under **Appliances, Furniture, & Furnishings**.

Included here, along with bedding and some miscellaneous items typically found in the bedroom, are things we tend to keep in our closets and drawers—namely clothes and accessories.

Some of the clothes and shoes in this inventory are listed in a general way. You probably want to make distinctions within certain categories to further define your own needs. A woman's casual shoes may mean loafers, flats, or moccasins to name just a few examples. Dresses can be casual, dressy, or formal and also vary according to the weather and seasons. Some men have quite a collection of hats and caps, reflecting not only seasonal needs, but also occupational choices or special interests.

Because there are more similarities than differences between adult's and children's clothing, all clothes are grouped together here even although not everything will apply to the young people.

Bedroom (Including Clothes)

Bedding

- ☐ Pillows
- ☐ Mattress Pads
- ☐ Sheets (Fitted & Top)
- ☐ Pillow Cases
- ☐ Blankets
- ☐ Bedcover (i.e., Bedspread, Quilt, Comforter or Comforter Set)
- ☐ Duvet & Duvet Cover
- ☐ Extra Pillows & Shams
- ☐ Throw Pillows
- ☐ Reading Pillow/Back Rest
- ☐ Clock
- ☐ Radio or Clock Radio
- ☐ Closet Organizers and/or Space Savers
- ☐ Under-the-Bed Storage Unit
- ☐ Garment Bags
- ☐ Assorted Clothes Hangers (i.e., Regular, Skirt, Slacks, Suit, Coat)
- ☐ Shoe Racks and/or Hangers
- ☐ Clothes Hamper or Basket
- ☐ Tie Rack
- ☐ Belt Rack
- ☐ Extra Clothing Hooks (Screw-type or Stick-on)
- ☐ Cedar Chips or Blocks for Closets
- ☐ Dresser Organizer (for Keys, Change, etc.)
- ☐ Jewelry Box

Jewelry

- ☐ Rings
- ☐ Bracelets
- ☐ Watches
- ☐ Necklaces and/or Chains
- ☐ Pendants
- ☐ Pins/Brooches
- ☐ Earrings
- ☐ Scarf Holders
- ☐ Tie Clips
- ☐ Cufflinks
- ☐ Money Clip
- ☐ Jewelry Cleaner
- ☐ Shoe Horn
- ☐ Extra Shoe Laces
- ☐ "Keepers" (Shoulder Strap Guards)
- ☐ Safety Pins, Assorted Sizes
- ☐ Full Length Mirror

Women's and Girls' Clothes & Accessories

Shoes

- ☐ Sneakers
- ☐ Casual
- ☐ Dress
- ☐ Sandals
- ☐ Boots
- ☐ Slippers
- ☐ Nylons (Hosiery)
- ☐ Knee Highs
- ☐ Socks
- ☐ Underpants
- ☐ Control Briefs & Body Shapers

- [ ] Bras
- [ ] Camisoles
- [ ] Slips
- [ ] Teddy and/or Other Special Lingerie
- [ ] Thermal Underwear
- [ ] Tights
- [ ] Nightgowns and/or Pajamas
- [ ] Bathrobes
- [ ] Bed jacket
- [ ] Jeans
- [ ] Casual Pants
- [ ] Dress Slacks
- [ ] Shorts
- [ ] Skirts
- [ ] Vests
- [ ] Suits
- [ ] Dresses (i.e., Casual, Daytime, Cocktail, Formal)
- [ ] Blouses (i.e., Long Sleeve, Short Sleeve)
- [ ] Shirts & Tops (i.e., Turtleneck, T-shirt, Polo)
- [ ] Sweaters (Cardigan & Pullover)
- [ ] Blazers
- [ ] Sweatshirts
- [ ] Sweatpants
- [ ] Jogging/Exercise/Sports Outfits
- [ ] Jackets (i.e., Windbreaker, All-Weather Coat, Parka)
- [ ] Coats (i.e., Rain, Heavy, Dress)
- [ ] Poncho, Shawl, Miscellaneous Wraps

- [ ] Uniforms
- [ ] Belts
- [ ] Purses
- [ ] Scarves and/or Ties
- [ ] Handkerchiefs
- [ ] Gloves
- [ ] Mittens
- [ ] Mufflers
- [ ] Hats
- [ ] Bathing Suits
- [ ] Bathing Suit Cover-up

Men's and Boys' Clothes & Accessories

Shoes

- [ ] Sneakers
- [ ] Casual
- [ ] Dress
- [ ] Thongs, Sandals, and/or Huaraches
- [ ] Slippers
- [ ] Boots
- [ ] Socks (Athletic & Dress)
- [ ] Underpants
- [ ] Athletic Supporters
- [ ] Undershirts
- [ ] Thermal Underwear
- [ ] Jeans
- [ ] Casual Pants
- [ ] Slacks
- [ ] Shorts
- [ ] Dress Shirts (i.e., Long Sleeve, Short Sleeve)
- [ ] Sports Shirts (i.e., Turtleneck, T-shirt, Polo/Golf)

- ☐ Flannel or Wool Shirts or Jackets
- ☐ Sweatshirts
- ☐ Sweatpants
- ☐ Sweaters
- ☐ Suits
- ☐ Sport coats
- ☐ Vests
- ☐ Jackets (i.e., Windbreaker, All-Weather Coat, Parka)
- ☐ Poncho
- ☐ Raincoat
- ☐ Overcoat
- ☐ Uniform
- ☐ Coveralls

- ☐ Formal Wear (Tuxedo & Accessories)
- ☐ Jogging or Exercise Outfits
- ☐ Pajamas
- ☐ Bathrobe
- ☐ Belts
- ☐ Suspenders
- ☐ Ties
- ☐ String Ties/Bolos
- ☐ Handkerchiefs
- ☐ Gloves
- ☐ Mufflers
- ☐ Scarves
- ☐ Hats & Caps

Chapter 15

Bathroom

The bathroom typically contains the things we use to keep ourselves clean, well-groomed, and healthy. This list reflects those essentials, plus it adds miscellaneous items that we tend to keep in this room. Some medications and first aid supplies are listed here, and you will find an additional list in the "First Aid Kit" in the **Emergency Supplies** chapter.

Bathroom

- ☐ Hamper
- ☐ Water-saving Devices for Shower, Sink Faucet, & Toilet
- ☐ Drinking Glass
- ☐ Bath Towels
- ☐ Hand Towels
- ☐ Guest Towels
- ☐ Wash Cloths
- ☐ Bath Sponge
- ☐ Bath Mat(s)
- ☐ Soap Dish
- ☐ Bath Soap
- ☐ Face Soap
- ☐ Astringent, Mask & Scrub
- ☐ Facial Sponge
- ☐ Liquid Soap & Pump Dispenser
- ☐ Bubble Bath and/or Bath Oil
- ☐ Shampoo
- ☐ Conditioner

- ☐ Haircolor Products
- ☐ Shower Caps
- ☐ Razor
- ☐ Razor Blades
- ☐ Shaving Cream
- ☐ Electric Razor
- ☐ Pre-shave
- ☐ After-shave
- ☐ Cologne and/or Perfume
- ☐ Body Lotion
- ☐ Hand Lotion
- ☐ Moisturizer or Other Face Cream
- ☐ Tooth Brushes
- ☐ Toothbrush Holders
- ☐ Toothbrush Covers
- ☐ Tooth Paste
- ☐ Mouthwash
- ☐ Dental Floss
- ☐ Tooth/Mouth Pain Relief Gel
- ☐ Orthodontic Aids (i.e., Rubber Bands, Wax, Retainers & Containers, Headgear)
- ☐ Combs
- ☐ Brushes
- ☐ Styling Gel or Mousse
- ☐ Water Bottle with Sprayer
- ☐ Hair Spray
- ☐ Blow Dryer and/or Diffuser
- ☐ Curling Iron
- ☐ Curlers
- ☐ Perm Rods
- ☐ Hair Clips and/or Curl Clips

- ☐ Bobby Pins
- ☐ Barrettes
- ☐ Ponytail Holders
- ☐ Head Bands
- ☐ Misc. Hair Accessories
- ☐ Hair Cutting Scissors
- ☐ Deodorant
- ☐ Bath Powder
- ☐ Petroleum Jelly
- ☐ Lip Balm

Make-up

- ☐ Lipstick
- ☐ Base and/or Cover-up
- ☐ Blush (Powder and/or Cream)
- ☐ Mascara
- ☐ Eyeliner (With Sharpener)
- ☐ Eye Shadow
- ☐ Powder
- ☐ Miscellaneous Cosmetics & Skin Care Products
- ☐ Cotton Balls
- ☐ Cotton Swabs (i.e., Q-tips)
- ☐ Baby Oil
- ☐ Tweezers
- ☐ Nail Scissors
- ☐ Nail Clippers
- ☐ Nail File and/or Emery Boards
- ☐ Cuticle Softener
- ☐ Nail Polish Remover
- ☐ Clear Nail Polish
- ☐ Nail Polish
- ☐ Nail Glue
- ☐ Nail Brush

Feminine Supplies
- ☐ Panty Liners
- ☐ Sanitary Pads
- ☐ Tampons
- ☐ Douche
- ☐ Lubricating Jelly
- ☐ Contraceptives
- ☐ Fever Thermometer (Oral, Rectal, and/or Other)
- ☐ Prescription Medicines (Oral & Topical)
- ☐ Aspirin and/or Similar Medication
- ☐ Cold/Allergy/Sinus Medicine
- ☐ Nasal Spray
- ☐ Eye Drops
- ☐ Ear Drops
- ☐ Anti-diarrhea Medicine
- ☐ Laxative
- ☐ Sleeping Aids
- ☐ Relaxants
- ☐ Rubbing Alcohol
- ☐ Witch Hazel
- ☐ Hydrogen Peroxide
- ☐ Band-Aids, Assorted Sizes & Shapes
- ☐ Topical Antibacterial Product (i.e., Providence Iodine)
- ☐ Bactine or Similar
- ☐ Anti-itch Lotion or Cream
- ☐ Pain Relieving Rub (i.e., Ben-Gay)

- ☐ Sunscreen
- ☐ Mosquito Repellant
- ☐ Contact Lens Solution
- ☐ Contact Lens Container
- ☐ Extra Contact Lenses
- ☐ Hand Mirror
- ☐ Vanity Tray
- ☐ Cupboard & Drawer Organizers
- ☐ Shower Caddy
- ☐ Clothing or Towel Hooks (Screw-type or Stick-on)
- ☐ Water Stopper & Plugs
- ☐ Scale for Weighing
- ☐ Toilet Paper
- ☐ Tissues
- ☐ Small Tissue Packets
- ☐ Night Light & Bulbs

Cleaning Supplies
- ☐ Toilet Bowl Brush
- ☐ Pumice
- ☐ Cleansers & Cleaning Products for Toilet, Sink, Shower and/or Bathtub, & Mirror
- ☐ Sponge and/or Cloth
- ☐ Plumber's Helper/Plunger
- ☐ Drain Opener
- ☐ Disinfectant (Liquid or Spray)
- ☐ Air Freshener
- ☐ Potpourri
- ☐ Candles & Matches

Chapter 16

The Laundry Area

(Including Cleaning Equipment & Supplies)

Not every home has a laundry room or area, but virtually everyone has dirty laundry and needs laundry supplies. Cleaning equipment and products are also listed here because they are at least somewhat related by the nature of their purpose, which is to clean. When brand names are used, they should not be taken as endorsements.

The Laundry Area

☐ Laundry Detergent

☐ Laundry Soap for Fine Washables (Powder and/or Liquid)

☐ Powdered Bleach

☐ Liquid Bleach

☐ Fabric Softener (Liquid or Sheets)

☐ Measuring Cup

☐ Stain Remover (Spray or Stick)

☐ Laundry Basket(s)

☐ Laundry Bag(s)

☐ Iron

☐ Ironing Board

☐ Ironing Board Pad & Cover

☐ Ironing Board Caddy

☐ Bottled Water

☐ Measuring Cup for Ironing Water

☐ Spray Bottle

☐ Starch and/or Fabric Sizing

- ☐ Clothes Brush
- ☐ Lint Pick-up
- ☐ Spot Remover (Dry Cleaning Type)
- ☐ Wall Tree
- ☐ Hanger Holder, Hooks, Racks & Organizers
- ☐ Clothes Line
- ☐ Clothes Pins
- ☐ Clothes Hangers
- ☐ Fabric Protector Spray for Clothes and Home Furnishings

Cleaning Equipment & Products

- ☐ Bucket and/or Pan
- ☐ Broom
- ☐ Dust Mop
- ☐ Mop
- ☐ Carpet Sweeper
- ☐ Vacuum Cleaner & Attachments
- ☐ Vacuum Cleaner Bags
- ☐ Electric Broom
- ☐ Carpet Cleaner
- ☐ Floor Polisher
- ☐ Whisk Broom
- ☐ Dust Pan
- ☐ Cordless Vac (i.e., Dustbuster)
- ☐ Cleaning/Polishing Rags, Assorted Sizes & Textures
- ☐ Sponges
- ☐ Scrub Brushes
- ☐ Feather Duster

- ☐ All-purpose Duster with Extender-type Handle to reach ceilings (i.e., Webster)
- ☐ All-purpose Spray Cleaner
- ☐ All-purpose Cleaner/Water Softener with Trisodium Phosphate (i.e., TSP)
- ☐ Ammonia
- ☐ Window Cleaner
- ☐ Degreaser
- ☐ Oven Cleaner
- ☐ Oil Soap for Wood
- ☐ Floor Cleaner for Linoleum-type Floors
- ☐ Floor Polish and/or Wax (Varies According to Type of Floor)
- ☐ Carpet Spotter
- ☐ Carpet Shampoo
- ☐ Furniture Polish, Wax, and/or Oil
- ☐ Mineral Oil
- ☐ Scratch Remover/Cover-up
- ☐ White Toothpaste
- ☐ Silver Polish
- ☐ Metal Polishes (i.e., Brass, Copper)
- ☐ Shoe/Boot Polishes and Creams
- ☐ Water Repellant Shoe Care Product
- ☐ Jewelry Cleaner
- ☐ Car Care Products (i.e., Shampoo, Wax, Chamois)
- ☐ Mop/Broom Organizer
- ☐ Miscellaneous Organizers, Racks, Hooks, etc.

Chapter 17

Office & School Supplies

More than 50 million Americans work from their homes at least part time, and about a quarter of those work at home full time. Many more Americans have carved out niches in their homes for managing their household finances, doing school homework, and pursuing hobbies. The lists here cover most of the things that relate to these and many other daily activities that are carried on in an average household. Look for "big ticket" items like desks, lamps, and a computer system elsewhere. Here you are more likely to find things to put in or on a desk.

A designated office space, especially, requires additional items that you can find in other chapters of this book, such as **Appliances, Furniture, & Furnishings**, **Electronics/ Technology**, and **Records, Documents, & The Safe Deposit Box**.

Office & School Supplies

Storage & Organizers

☐ Crates

☐ Drawer Storage (i.e., Cardboard, Mesh, Plastic)

☐ Desktop File Holders

☐ File Cabinets & Carts

☐ Record Storage Boxes

☐ Literature Holders (i.e., Desk, Floor, Wall Styles)

☐ Desk Pad

- ☐ Desk Caddy
- ☐ Business Card Holder
- ☐ Drawer Organizer
- ☐ Rolodex Card Organizer
- ☐ Index Card Box
- ☐ Bookends
- ☐ Bookshelves
- ☐ Magazine Files
- ☐ Supply Closet Organizers (i.e., Shelf-savers, Cubes, Bins)
- ☐ Binders (i.e., Presentation, Reference, Storage, Specialty)
- ☐ Index Dividers
- ☐ Report Covers
- ☐ Two-Pocket Portfolios
- ☐ File Folders
- ☐ Hanging File Folders
- ☐ File Jackets & Sorters
- ☐ Filing Accessories (i.e., Tabs & Inserts, Guides, Labels)
- ☐ Expandable Files
- ☐ Clip Boards

Paper
- ☐ Adding Machine/Calculator
- ☐ Binder
- ☐ Columnar Pads
- ☐ Computer
- ☐ Copy
- ☐ Graph
- ☐ Forms (i.e., Expense, Invoice, Sales & Purchase Orders, Shipping & Packing, Legal)
- ☐ Ledger

- ☐ Lined Paper Pads
- ☐ Letterhead
- ☐ Message Pads
- ☐ Note Cards
- ☐ Scratch
- ☐ Stationery, Assorted
- ☐ Typing
- ☐ Notebooks
- ☐ Index Cards
- ☐ Post-It Notes
- ☐ Business Cards
- ☐ Label Makers & Printers
- ☐ Labels (i.e., Filing ID & Specialty, Media, Cards & Badges)
- ☐ Bank Checks & Deposit Slips
- ☐ Adding Machine
- ☐ Calculator
- ☐ Cash Box/Drawer
- ☐ Coin Tray
- ☐ Coin counter
- ☐ Coin & Bill Wrappers
- ☐ Safe

Mailroom Equipment & Supplies
- ☐ Postage Meters
- ☐ Shipping & Postal Scales
- ☐ Envelopes, Assorted
- ☐ Packing Material
- ☐ Mailing Tape
- ☐ Shipping & Mailing Labels
- ☐ Address Stamp with Pad
- ☐ Letter Opener

- ☐ Postage Stamps
- ☐ Post Cards
- ☐ Address Books & Directories
- ☐ Phone Book(s)

Writing Supplies

- ☐ Pens
- ☐ Pencils
- ☐ Erasers
- ☐ Colored Pens, Marking Pens, and/or Pencils
- ☐ Indelible Ink Pen
- ☐ Highlighters
- ☐ Correction Fluid and/or Tape
- ☐ Pencil Sharpener
- ☐ Scissors
- ☐ X-Acto & Utility Knife
- ☐ Stapler & Staples
- ☐ Staple Gun & Staples
- ☐ Staple Puller
- ☐ Paper Clips
- ☐ Specialty Clips & Fasteners
- ☐ Rubber Bands
- ☐ Ruler
- ☐ Protractor
- ☐ Compass
- ☐ Hole Puncher
- ☐ Gummed Reinforcements for Holed Paper
- ☐ Scotch Tape
- ☐ Glue & Adhesive Products
- ☐ Calendar (i.e., Desk, Wall, Planner)
- ☐ Appointment Book/Daytimer
- ☐ Bulletin Board
- ☐ Push Pins
- ☐ Thumb Tacks
- ☐ Dry-Erase Board
- ☐ Presentation Easel & Paper
- ☐ Brief Case
- ☐ Totes
- ☐ Portfolio
- ☐ Catalog Case
- ☐ Computer Backpack
- ☐ Computer Cases & Bags
- ☐ Ergonomic Equipment (i.e., Work Station, Desktop Holders, Footrest)
- ☐ Chair mats
- ☐ Typewriter, Spare Ribbons & Correcting Ribbons

Chapter 18

Outdoor Living &
Maintenance

The outdoor areas of our homes can almost be
considered as additional rooms in the
sense that our patios, decks, and gardens
offer other spaces for eating, relaxing, playing, and working. These spaces can be extensions of our indoor lifestyles and often require
their own furniture, furnishings, and maintenance
equipment.

The following lists reflect the work, play, and aesthetics we
associate with outdoor living.

Outdoor Living and Maintenance

On or Around the Home

☐ Mailbox

☐ Address Sign & Number

☐ Name Plaque

☐ Door Knocker

☐ Doormats

☐ Outdoor Thermometer

☐ Windchimes

☐ Weathervane

☐ Outdoor Decorations

☐ National and/or State Flag & Holder(s)

☐ Birdfeeder & Birdfeed

☐ Birdhouse

☐ Birdbath

☐ Garden Lamps

☐ Statues

☐ Garbage & Recycle Cans

114

☐ Planter Boxes & Liners
☐ Pots & Seed-starters

Outdoor Living & Dining

☐ Tables (i.e., Picnic Style, Small, Utility Type)
☐ Umbrella
☐ Heater
☐ Chairs
☐ Chaise Lounge
☐ Bench
☐ Cushion
☐ Hammock
☐ Play Equipment
☐ Portable Folding Chairs
☐ Barbecue
☐ Smoker Attachment
☐ Rotisserie
☐ Drip Pan Liners
☐ Ash Catcher
☐ Barbecue cover
☐ Barbecue Table or Cart
☐ Fuel (i.e., Charcoal, Propane)
☐ Charcoal Funnel
☐ Charcoal Companion
☐ Lighter Fluid
☐ Electric Starter
☐ Spray Bottle or Squirt Gun
☐ Long-handled Tongs, Spatula, Fork
☐ Skewers
☐ Basting Brush
☐ Grilling Basket
☐ Wire Barbecue-Cleaning Brush

☐ Heavy Potholders and/or Mitts
☐ Tablecloth(s)
☐ Apron
☐ Citronella Candles
☐ Unbreakable Glasses & Dishes
☐ Paper Plates
☐ Paper Plate Holders/Baskets
☐ Large Ice Chest
☐ Wine Cooling Containers

The Picnic

☐ Ground Cloth
☐ Picnic Basket
☐ Ice Chest
☐ "Blue Ice"
☐ Utility Knife with Can Opener & Cork Screw
☐ Reusable/Recyclable Plastic Cups & Utensils
☐ Portable Folding Chairs (i.e., Beach)

Outdoor & Garden Maintenance

☐ Broom
☐ Dust Pan
☐ Rake
☐ Hoe
☐ Cultivator
☐ Shovel
☐ Snow Shovel
☐ Trowel & Other Digging Tools
☐ Trash Bags
☐ Trash Can

☐ Ladder
☐ Gardening Gloves
☐ Gardening Clippers
☐ Pruning Tools (i.e., Shears, Saw, Lopper, Pole, Pruner)
☐ Hedge Trimmer
☐ Lawn Mower
☐ Lawn Mower Bag
☐ Edger
☐ Lawn Aerator
☐ Lawn Spreader
☐ Weed Eater
☐ Leaf Blower
☐ Wheelbarrow or Utility Cart
☐ Bucket
☐ Watering Can
☐ Gardening Stakes & Ties
☐ Potting Soil
☐ Plant Food
☐ Fertilizer
☐ Fertilizer Spreader
☐ Composter
☐ Compost Tools
☐ Tree Seal

☐ Weed Killer
☐ Snail & Slug Bait
☐ Ant & Insect Poison
☐ Garden Hose(s)
☐ Hose Reel(s)
☐ Decorative Faucet Handles
☐ Water Nozzle Sprayer
☐ Portable Sprinklers (i.e., Rainbird)
☐ Automatic Timer(s) for Sprinklers

Swimming Pool/Spa Equipment & Supplies
☐ Pool Thermometer
☐ Leaf Scoop
☐ Pool Sweep
☐ Brushes (Hand-held & Long Handle)
☐ Water-testing Kit
☐ Pool Chemicals
☐ Toys
☐ Floats (i.e., Kick Board, Raft, Life Jackets, Water Wings)

Chapter 19

Storage Spaces — Small & Large

Storage covers a lot of territory, both literally and figuratively. It refers to the kinds of spaces where we keep things that aren't in constant use. It includes all sorts of things that are not particularly related to other items on the list, except that they are all things that can be put away.

Some of the items here appear on other lists but are included in this section because they are often stored out of sight and not necessarily in the rooms with which they are generally associated. Table leaves and pads, for instance, are not usually in use in the dining room. More often than not, they are in a closet somewhere else awaiting a dinner party.

Some of the items listed here are whole categories in themselves and have their own separate chapters. When that is the case, the items are preceded by an asterisk and followed by a note in parentheses directing you to that chapter. For example, *Luggage & Other Travel Items will say (see **Travel**).

This section is divided into two parts. Although certain items are somewhat arbitrarily placed in one part or the other, the idea is that we tend to keep some of our things in closets, cupboards, and drawers while we store others in larger spaces (if we have them) like garages, basements, attics, or sheds.

I. Closets, Spare Cupboards, & Drawers

- ☐ Extra Bedding & Pillows
- ☐ Extra Towels & Miscellaneous Linens
- ☐ Beach Towels
- ☐ Sleeping Bags
- ☐ Backpacks
- ☐ Table Leaves & Pads
- ☐ Portable Sewing Machine

Sewing Kit

- ☐ Pin Cushion
- ☐ Straight Pins
- ☐ Needles
- ☐ Needle Threader
- ☐ Safety Pins
- ☐ Sewing Machine Needles & Oil
- ☐ Bobbins
- ☐ Thread, Assorted
- ☐ Scissors
- ☐ Pinking Shears
- ☐ Embroidery Scissors
- ☐ Thimble
- ☐ Crochet Hook
- ☐ Seam Ripper
- ☐ Tailor's Chalk
- ☐ Measuring Tape
- ☐ Patches
- ☐ Indelible Ink Marking Pen
- ☐ Name Labels
- ☐ Hooks & Eyes
- ☐ Snaps
- ☐ Elastic
- ☐ Extra Buttons
- ☐ Seam Binding
- ☐ Material Scraps
- ☐ Humidifier/Vaporizer
- ☐ Heating Pad
- ☐ Ice Pack
- ☐ Fly Swatter
- ☐ Yard Stick
- ☐ Light Bulbs, Assorted
- ☐ Flashlights
- ☐ Candles
- ☐ Candle Holders
- ☐ Batteries, Assorted
- ☐ Battery Tester
- ☐ Battery Recharger
- ☐ Extension Cords
- ☐ Plug Extenders
- ☐ Automatic Light Timers
- ☐ String
- ☐ Twine
- ☐ Rope
- ☐ Wire
- ☐ Bungee Cords

Tape

- ☐ Scotch
- ☐ Mailing
- ☐ Strapping
- ☐ Masking
- ☐ Duct
- ☐ Paste

Glue

- ☐ Mucilage
- ☐ All-purpose
- ☐ Household Cement
- ☐ Wood Glue

☐ Glue Stick
☐ Super Glue
☐ Picture Hooks & Holders
☐ Tacks
☐ Umbrellas
☐ Binoculars
☐ Camera
☐ Film
☐ Photograph Albums
☐ Containers, "Frogs" & Oasis for Plants & Flowers
☐ Watering Can with Spout for House Plants
☐ Boxes, Assorted Sizes to Hold Miscellaneous Odds & Ends
☐ Gift Boxes, Assorted Sizes & Shapes
☐ Gift Wrapping Paper
☐ Tissue Paper
☐ Ribbons & Bows
☐ Gift Cards and/or Tags
☐ Greeting Cards
☐ Coupon Organizer
☐ Maps
☐ Magnifying Glass
☐ Spare Reading Glasses
☐ Eye Glass Cord or Chain
☐ Eye Glass Repair Kit
☐ Sun Glasses
☐ Lining Material for Shelves, Drawers & Cupboards
☐ Sachet for Drawers
☐ Color Palette or Swatches (for those who have had their colors done)
☐ Miscellaneous Decorative

Items & Bric-a-Brac
☐ Ashtrays
☐ Door Stops
☐ Hobby Items & Collections (See **"The Arts, Hobbies, & Collections"**)
☐ Costumes

II. The Garage, Basement, Attic, & Shed

Tools
☐ Tool Box
☐ Bucket Buddy
☐ Trouble Light
☐ Extra Bright Flashlights
☐ Measuring Tape
☐ Level
☐ Tri-Square
☐ Carpenter's Square
☐ Hammer(s)
☐ Screwdrivers (Regular & Phillips, Assorted Sizes)
☐ Pliers (Needlenose & Others)
☐ Wirecutter
☐ Crescent Wrench
☐ Allen Wrench Set
☐ Chisel
☐ Nail Set
☐ Set of Files
☐ Electrician's Tape
☐ Duct Tape
☐ Wire
☐ Handsaw
☐ Hacksaw
☐ Crowbar/Prybar

☐ Razor
☐ Scraper
☐ Utility Knife
☐ Putty Knife
☐ C-clamps
☐ Socket Set
☐ Drill & Drill Bits
☐ Epoxy Cement
☐ Heavy-duty Extension Cord
☐ Assortment of Nails, Nuts, Screws, Woodscrews, & Washers
☐ Electric Tools (i.e., Screwdriver, Sander, Drill, Jigsaw, etc.)
☐ Ladder (i.e., Folding Step, Extension)
☐ Handtruck and/or Dolly
☐ Saw Horses
☐ Fire Extinguisher (A-B-C Rating)
☐ Filters for Furnace and/or Air Conditioner
☐ Cleaning Equipment & Products (See **The Laundry Area**)

Miscellaneous Home Maintenance Supplies

☐ Paint
☐ Paint Thinner
☐ Paint Brushes
☐ Paint Gun
☐ Mortar
☐ Caulking
☐ Patching Plaster
☐ Spackling

☐ Carpenter's Wood Filler
☐ Stipple
☐ Sandpaper
☐ Steel Wool
☐ Abrasive Nylon Pads
☐ Household Oil
☐ Squeak Stopper (i.e., WD-40)
☐ Car Equipment & Supplies (See **The Car**)
☐ Camping & Backpacking Equipment (See **Camping & Backpacking**)
☐ Sporting Goods & Exercise Equipment (See **Recreation, Sports, & Exercise**)
☐ Luggage & Other Travel Items (See **Travel**)
☐ Plant Food, Fertilizer & Potting Soil
☐ Firewood
☐ Kindling
☐ Firewood Carrier
☐ Oil Lamps
☐ Lamp Oil
☐ Emergency & First Aid Supplies (See **Emergency Supplies**)
☐ Medical Supplies/Convalescent Equipment
☐ Storage Organizers, Caddies, Drawers, Baskets, Racks, S Racks, Hooks & Clips, Peg Board & Parts Bins
☐ Hobby Items & Collections (See **The Arts, Hobbies, & Collections**)

Chapter 20

Emergency Supplies

All of us, no matter where we live, are subject to threats of one kind of disaster or another. We should, therefore, keep enough emergency supplies on hand to last us a few days in case we are left to our own devices. The following list is an attempt to meet that need.

Included in the list is a first aid kit. Items in the kit should be kept together because they are an important part of emergency supplies. However, items for a first aid kit include many of the everyday things that we usually keep in our bathrooms and kitchens. You may want to put together a separate first aid kit to keep in your car or to take on trips.

Water, canned or packaged foods, and medications should be checked periodically to make sure that dates haven't expired.

Emergency Supplies

☐ Container(s) to Hold Emergency Supplies (i.e., Trash Cans, Bins, Backpacks)

☐ Bottled Water (2 Qts. to 2 Gals. Per Person Per Day; 2-Week Supply)

☐ To sanitize water: Heat to a rolling boil for at least 5 minutes, or add 16 drops of bleach per gallon of water. Stir and let sit for 30 minutes.

☐ Sterilized, Purified Pouches of Water

☐ Canned Juices

121

Food (At Least 5 Day Supply Per Person)

- ☐ Packaged, Canned, Dehydrated Assortment
- ☐ Food Bars
- ☐ Juices
- ☐ Milk, Rice or Soy Milk (Powdered or Canned)
- ☐ Food for Infants and/or Pets

Cooking & Eating Utensils

- ☐ Barbecue, Camp Stove, Hibachi
- ☐ Fuel
- ☐ Matches in Waterproof Container
- ☐ Pot or Pan
- ☐ Stirring/Serving Spoon
- ☐ Sharp Knife
- ☐ Portable Can Opener
- ☐ Nonbreakable Plates, Bowls, and Cups
- ☐ Knives, Forks, and Spoons
- ☐ Paper Towels
- ☐ Heavy-duty Aluminum Foil
- ☐ Wash Pan
- ☐ Dish Soap
- ☐ Flashlight and Extra Batteries
- ☐ Portable Radio & Extra Batteries
- ☐ Whistle (To call for help)
- ☐ Tools (i.e., Wrench to turn off utilities, Hammer, Pliers, Screwdrivers, Ax, Prybar)

Information

- ☐ Map of Area
- ☐ Directions to Local Hospitals & Emergency Relief Centers
- ☐ Telephone Numbers of Local Police, Fire Department, and Hospital
- ☐ Contact Person (Preferably out of state) with whom family members can check
- ☐ Personal Directories (i.e., Phone Numbers, e-mail Addresses)

Sanitary Supplies

- ☐ Bucket with Tight Lid
- ☐ Toilet Paper
- ☐ Large Plastic Bags with Ties
- ☐ Small Shovel
- ☐ Disinfectant (i.e., Powdered Chlorinated Lime) or Bleach
- ☐ Deodorizer
- ☐ Newspaper to Wrap Garbage & Waste
- ☐ Pre-moistened Towelettes
- ☐ Feminine & Infant Supplies
- ☐ Hand Sanitizer
- ☐ Bar Soap
- ☐ Liquid Detergent
- ☐ Shampoo
- ☐ Toothpaste
- ☐ Toothbrushes

- ☐ Ground Cloth
- ☐ Tent
- ☐ Blankets (Insulated, All-weather Thermal)
- ☐ Change of Clothing (Include Rain Gear)
- ☐ Sturdy Shoes
- ☐ Protective Hat or Cap
- ☐ Plastic Sheeting
- ☐ Duct Tape
- ☐ Staple Gun
- ☐ Dust Masks
- ☐ Work Gloves
- ☐ Coil of 1/2″ Rope
- ☐ Coil of Baling Wire
- ☐ Fire Extinguisher (A-B-C)
- ☐ Compass
- ☐ Scissors
- ☐ Candles & Waterproof Matches
- ☐ Cash (Small Bills & Change for Telephone & Traveler's Checks)
- ☐ Paper, Pencils, Pens
- ☐ Books, Magazines, Games, Toys

First Aid Kit

- ☐ First Aid Instruction Handbook
- ☐ Writing Materials (i.e. Paper, Pencils, Pens)
- ☐ Prescription and/or Other Special Medicine
- ☐ Pain Relief Medication (i.e., Aspirin, Ibuprofen)

- ☐ Scissors
- ☐ Tweezers & Needle
- ☐ Rubbing Alcohol Preps
- ☐ Hydogen Peroxide
- ☐ Antibacterial Solution (i.e., Providine Iodine)
- ☐ Baking Soda
- ☐ Table Salt
- ☐ Antacids
- ☐ Cough Mixture
- ☐ Throat Lozenges
- ☐ Diarrhea Medication
- ☐ Laxative
- ☐ Ear Drops
- ☐ Toothache Remedy
- ☐ Motion Sickness Tablets (For nausea)
- ☐ Topical Ointment
- ☐ Box of Plastic Strips (i.e., Band-Aids), Assorted Sizes
- ☐ Clean Sheet (To use for Bandages)
- ☐ Rolls of Adhesive Tape (2″ & 4″ Wide, Hypoallergenic)
- ☐ Sterile Gauze
- ☐ 4″ x 4″ Sterile Dressing Pads (24)
- ☐ Triangular Bandages
- ☐ Sterile Cotton
- ☐ ABD or Sanitary Pads
- ☐ 24″ Ace Bandage Wrap
- ☐ Splints (18″ Wooden)
- ☐ Cotton Swabs
- ☐ Safety Pins, Assorted Sizes

- ☐ Fever Thermometer(s)
- ☐ Eyedropper
- ☐ Water Purification Materials
- ☐ Collapsible or Paper Cups
- ☐ Waterproof Matches
- ☐ 2 Quick Cold Packs
- ☐ Resealable, Waterproof Bags
- ☐ Latex Gloves

Chapter 21

Infants & Toddlers

Both infants and toddlers use many of the items listed here, but some items on the list are best suited for either one or the other. Although the items are fairly well interspersed, there are more infant items toward the beginning of the list and more toddler things at the end.

Infants & Toddlers

- ☐ Crib with Waterproof Mattress
- ☐ Bumper Pads
- ☐ Waterproof Mattress Pads
- ☐ Fitted Sheets
- ☐ Blankets/Quilts/Comforters
- ☐ Dressing Table & Pad
- ☐ Chest of Drawers
- ☐ Portacrib
- ☐ Travel Sleeper & Bedding
- ☐ Cradle/Bassinet
- ☐ Activity Mat
- ☐ Play Yard & Pad
- ☐ Baby Bath
- ☐ Reclining Infant Seat
- ☐ Auto Safety Seat
- ☐ Collapsible Stroller
- ☐ Pram/Baby Carriage
- ☐ Baby Carrier (Back, Front, or Sling) for Parents
- ☐ Highchair or Feeding Table
- ☐ Booster Seat
- ☐ Swing
- ☐ Bouncer
- ☐ Child-Size Table & Chairs

☐ Rocking Chair or Glider
☐ Step Chair
☐ Nursing Stool
☐ Potty Training Chair/Seat
☐ Diapers
☐ Waterproof Pants
☐ Diaper Stacker
☐ Diaper Bag
☐ Diaper Pail & Deodorizers
☐ Lap Pads
☐ Burp Cloths

Layette Items
☐ Receiving Blankets
☐ Washcloths
☐ Hooded Towels
☐ After-bath Bags
☐ Snapside Shirts
☐ Diaper Covers
☐ Gowns
☐ Bodysuits
☐ Stretchies
☐ Coming Home Outfit
☐ Bunting
☐ Coveralls
☐ Pullover Shirts
☐ Bibs
☐ Booties & Baby Shoes
☐ Socks
☐ Cap or Bonnet
☐ Sweater Sets
☐ Sterilizer with Bottle Nurser Set
☐ Breast Pump Set
☐ Food Grinder

☐ Food Tray
☐ Placemat
☐ Unbreakable Bowls
☐ Unbreakable Spillproof Cup with Lid
☐ Baby Spoons
☐ Pacifiers (Orthodontic)

Nursery Accessories
☐ Baby Monitor
☐ Mobile
☐ Crib Skirt
☐ Canopy
☐ Crib Pillow
☐ Crib Toys
☐ Toy Chest
☐ Hamper
☐ Nursery Scale
☐ Lamp
☐ Switchplate
☐ Wallhangings/Pictures/ Plaques
☐ Stuffed Animals
☐ Rattle
☐ Teething Ring/Toys
☐ Bath Toys
☐ Cloth Books

Personal Care Items
☐ Soap
☐ Antibacterial Cleanser
☐ Shampoo
☐ Oil
☐ Lotion
☐ Sunscreen
☐ Diaper Rash Ointment

☐ Premoistened Towelettes and/or Diaper Wipes

☐ Diaper Liners

☐ Nail Scissors

☐ Hair Brush & Comb

☐ Thermometer (i.e., Ear or Forehead)

☐ Nasal Syringe

☐ Cotton Balls

☐ Cotton Swabs

☐ Tissues

☐ Baby Laundry Detergent

☐ Humidifier/Vaporizer/Air Purifier

☐ Baby Record Book

☐ Photograph Albums

☐ Parenting Books

☐ Books/Picture Books

☐ Board Books

☐ Toys

☐ Bath Toys

☐ Baskets &/or Bins

☐ Lightweight Balls (i.e. Nerf, Whiffle)

Safety Equipment

☐ Guardrail

☐ Expandable Security Gates

☐ Electrical Outlet Plugs or Guards

☐ Door Knob Covers

☐ Door Locks

☐ Cabinet Door Locks and/or Safety Catches

☐ Medicine Cabinet Locks

☐ Locks for Toilet, Oven, Refrigerator

☐ Fireplace Lock or Screen

☐ Padding for Fireplace/Furniture

☐ Furniture Restraints (Attached to Furniture & Wall Studs)

☐ Drawer Stops

☐ Window Safety Locks

☐ Child Safety & Emergency Book

Clothing

☐ Socks

☐ Shoes

☐ Training Pants

☐ Underpants

☐ Undershirts

☐ Tights

☐ Pajamas

☐ Sleepers

☐ Coveralls

☐ Shirts/Blouses

☐ Dresses

☐ Sweaters

☐ Sweatshirts

☐ Jackets

☐ Caps/Hats/Bonnets

☐ Snowsuit

☐ Raingear

☐ Swim Diapers

☐ Swimsuit & Cover-Up

Chapter 22

Kids' Stuff

M ost of the things on this list apply primarily to young children, including older toddlers. Other items, like video games, balls, and a train set, may appeal to children of all ages. We don't have a separate list for school-age and older children because most of their belongings can be found in other chapters. School supplies, for instance, are included in the **Office & School Supplies** chapter, and clothes are covered in the **Bedroom** chapter. Many items listed in the **Recreation, Sports, & Exercise** and **Electronics/Technology** chapters are also applicable to older children.

Kids' Stuff

- ☐ Child-size Furniture (i.e., Table & Chairs, Rocking Chairs)
- ☐ Night Light
- ☐ Books
- ☐ Stuffed Animals
- ☐ Dolls
- ☐ Doll Accessories (i.e., Clothes, Furniture, House, Tea Set)
- ☐ Puppets
- ☐ Balls
- ☐ Frisbee
- ☐ Stacking & Shape-sorting Toys
- ☐ Building Toys (i.e., Blocks, Legos, Lincoln Logs, Tinkertoys)
- ☐ Platform Toys (i.e., Play Family, Post Office)
- ☐ Jack-in-the-Box

□ Top
□ Toy Cars & Trucks
□ Puzzles
□ Color Forms
□ Magnets (i.e., Alphabet)

Art Supplies
  □ Paper, Assorted
  □ Scissors
  □ Paste
  □ Glue
  □ Crayons
  □ Watercolors & Brushes
  □ Fingerpaint
  □ Easel
  □ Smock
  □ Clay
  □ Playdough

□ Musical Instruments
□ Tape Recorder & Cassette Tapes
□ CD Player & CDs
□ DVD Player & DVDs
□ Board Games
□ Electronic Games (i.e., Nintendo, Gameboy)
□ Video Games
□ Video Cassettes
□ Model Kits
□ Flashcards
□ Kites
□ Push Toys (i.e., Shopping Cart, Lawn Mower)
□ Pull Toys (Wagon, Animals)
□ Rocking Horse

□ Riding Toys without Pedals
□ Miniature House & Accessories
□ Train Set
□ Big Wheel or Other Riding Toys
□ Tricycle
□ Bicycle & Training Wheels
□ Bike Accessories (i.e., Basket, Bell or Horn)
□ Scooter
□ Skate Board
□ Roller Skates and/or Roller Blades
□ Inflatable Swimming Pool
□ Swing Set
□ Slide
□ Climbing Toys
□ Sand Box
□ Sand Toys (i.e., Bucket, Shovel)
□ Snow Toys (i.e., Sled, Inner Tube)
□ Travel Activity Games & Books
□ Piggy Bank
□ Backpack
□ Lunch Box and/or Lined Bag

Chapter 23

Pet Supplies

The following list will provide you with the basic supplies for the feeding, grooming, safety, and overall well-being of most common pets.

Pet Supplies

- ☐ Food & Water Dishes
- ☐ Placemat
- ☐ Pet Food
- ☐ Snack Food
- ☐ Automatic Pet Feeder
- ☐ Food Containers
- ☐ Vitamins & Minerals
- ☐ Skin or Other Supplements
- ☐ Medicine (Oral and/or Topical)
- ☐ Dental Care Products
- ☐ Things to Chew
- ☐ Shampoo
- ☐ Conditioner
- ☐ Sink Shower
- ☐ Pet Brush
- ☐ Pet Comb
- ☐ Nail Clippers & File
- ☐ Flea & Tick Powder, Spray, or Collar
- ☐ Collar, Tags & Reflector
- ☐ Choke Collar
- ☐ Small Dog Harness
- ☐ Leash
- ☐ Chain or Other Tether
- ☐ Portable Enclosure
- ☐ Invisible Fence with Receiver Collar
- ☐ Security Gate

- [ ] Car Barrier
- [ ] Pet Door
- [ ] "Pooper Scooper"
- [ ] Pet Hair Pick-up
- [ ] Dog Whistle
- [ ] House/Cage/Tank/Bowl
- [ ] Portable Kennel/Carrier
- [ ] Bed/Basket & Cushion
- [ ] Litter Box with Liner, Litter & Scoop
- [ ] Scratching Post
- [ ] Hamster Cage with Exercise Wheel
- [ ] Bedding Material for Hamsters, Gerbils & Pet Mice
- [ ] Bird Cage with Perches & Perch Cleaner
- [ ] Bird Bottle & Feeder
- [ ] Aquarium
- [ ] Aquarium Accessories (i.e., Air Pump, Light, Heater, Filter, Air Valve, Aerator Bar, Net, Airline Tubing, Thermometer, Filter Floss, Activated Carbon, Plants, Ornamental Items)
- [ ] Terrarium & Moss
- [ ] Reptile Cage Carpet, Rocks & Rock Warmer
- [ ] Toys
- [ ] Pet Literature (i.e., American Kennel Club Books; Training Manual)
- [ ] Medical Records
- [ ] Pedigree Papers

Chapter 24

Recreation, Sports, & Exercise

This chapter lists a wide range of recreational, sports, and exercise activities and the basic equipment needed for them. Most households probably have items for one or more of these categories but certainly not all or even most of them.

Some of the groupings may appear sparse, but that is intentional. Instead of listing every piece of clothing or equipment for every activity or sport, you will find some generic items listed at the top of the list. These items can be added to appropriate subsections when needed. Take the category of football, for instance. Theoretically, all you need are a ball and some players. But if you are on a team, you obviously need a number of the generic items, including a uniform and shoes with cleats.

Some kind of case or bag is useful, or even necessary, for a number of the items on the list. If that's true for your particular sport or activity, just add that to your list in this mix-and-match chapter.

Recreation, Sports, & Exercise

Generic Items That Apply or Can Be Adapted to Various Activities

- [ ] Hats, Caps, Helmets & Visors
- [ ] Clothes & Uniforms
- [ ] Raingear
- [ ] Shoes & Boots
- [ ] Shoe Repair Supplies (i.e., Shoe-Goo)
- [ ] Gloves
- [ ] Goggles
- [ ] Carrying Case
- [ ] Sports Bag
- [ ] Hip Pack
- [ ] Sweatband
- [ ] Wristband
- [ ] Shinguard
- [ ] Kneeguard
- [ ] Elbowguard
- [ ] Mouth Guard
- [ ] Sweat Towel
- [ ] Water Bottle
- [ ] Air Pump
- [ ] Instructional & Rule Books or Manuals

Archery

- [ ] Bows
- [ ] Arrows
- [ ] Quiver
- [ ] Target

Badminton

- [ ] Raquets
- [ ] Birdies
- [ ] Net

Baseball/Softball

- [ ] Bat
- [ ] Ball
- [ ] Mitt

Basketball

- [ ] Ball
- [ ] Backboard with Hoop & Net

Bicycling

- [ ] Bicycle
- [ ] Cable or Chain & Lock
- [ ] Bike Tool Set
- [ ] Basket
- [ ] Training Wheels for Beginners
- [ ] Rack

Billiards/Pool

- [ ] Table
- [ ] Balls
- [ ] Cue Sticks
- [ ] Bridge Head
- [ ] Triangle
- [ ] Chalk
- [ ] Table Brush
- [ ] Table Cover
- [ ] Cue Rack

Bocce

- [ ] Bocce Ball Set

Bowling
- ☐ Ball
- ☐ Resin/Powder

Boxing
- ☐ Gloves
- ☐ Punching Bag Set

Croquet
- ☐ Mallets
- ☐ Balls
- ☐ Goal Stakes
- ☐ Hoops

Darts
- ☐ Darts
- ☐ Dart Board

Exercise Equipment
- ☐ Floor Mat
- ☐ Exercise Machines (i.e., Stationary Bike, Treadmill, Rower)
- ☐ Trampoline
- ☐ Wrist & Ankle Weights

Fishing
- ☐ Rod
- ☐ Reel
- ☐ Tackle Box and/or Vest
- ☐ Hooks
- ☐ Fishing Lines
- ☐ Weights
- ☐ Bait and/or Lures or Flies
- ☐ Net
- ☐ Knife
- ☐ Fish Scaler
- ☐ Waders

Football
- ☐ Ball

Golf
- ☐ Clubs
- ☐ Bag
- ☐ Balls
- ☐ Tees
- ☐ Ball Markers
- ☐ Green Repair Tools
- ☐ Cart
- ☐ Club Covers
- ☐ Ball Retriever
- ☐ Umbrella

Horseshoes
- ☐ Horseshoes
- ☐ Pegs

Hunting/Shooting
- ☐ Gun Safe
- ☐ Gun
- ☐ Trigger Locks
- ☐ Scope
- ☐ Ammunition
- ☐ Targets
- ☐ Gun Cleaning Kit
- ☐ Gun Case
- ☐ Hunting Knife

Ping Pong/Table Tennis
- ☐ Table
- ☐ Net
- ☐ Paddles
- ☐ Balls

Raquetball
- ☐ Raquet
- ☐ Balls
- ☐ Raquet Cover

Skiing & Snowboarding
- ☐ Skis
- ☐ Poles
- ☐ Boots
- ☐ Boot Carrier
- ☐ After-ski Boots
- ☐ Ski Rack
- ☐ Snowboard

Soccer
- ☐ Ball

Swimming & Related
- ☐ Lifejacket
- ☐ Fins
- ☐ Water Socks
- ☐ Diving Mask/Goggles
- ☐ Ear Plugs
- ☐ Nose Plug
- ☐ Snorkel
- ☐ Wet Suit
- ☐ Kickboard
- ☐ Raft
- ☐ Water Skis
- ☐ Scuba Equipment
- ☐ Water Toys, Games, & Floats
- ☐ Swimmer's Towel/Chamois
- ☐ Beach Towels

Tennis
- ☐ Raquet
- ☐ Balls
- ☐ Raquet Cover and/or Press

Tetherball
- ☐ Tetherball Set

Volleyball
- ☐ Ball
- ☐ Net

Weightlifting
- ☐ Barbell/Dumbell Set
- ☐ Weight Bench

Yoga
- ☐ Mat

Miscellaneous
- ☐ Jump Rope
- ☐ Roller Skates
- ☐ Roller Blades
- ☐ Ice Skates
- ☐ Skateboard

Chapter 25

Travel

This chapter is not intended to be a definitive list for packing for a trip. It includes a number of items that aren't found in other lists in this book, although there is some duplication. You would probably take some of the items listed here on even the shortest trip, such as luggage and a cosmetic bag or shaving kit. You will need other items, such as a currency converter and foreign language dictionaries, only if you plan to travel out of the country.

The next chapter, **Camping & Backpacking**, also contains items that you may want to add to your travel list. There you will find things like sleeping bags, towels, and eating utensils, which are not included here. Also, many of the personal items that go in our cosmetic bags and shaving kits are not included in the following list.

Travel

Luggage
- ☐ Garment Bag
- ☐ 21″ to 29″ Pullman Cases
- ☐ Carry-on
- ☐ Tote Bag
- ☐ Duffel
- ☐ Satchel
- ☐ Train/Cosmetic Case
- ☐ Backpack
- ☐ Lightweight Folding Suitcase to Pack

- ☐ Luggage Tags Luggage Carrier (With Wheels & Cords)
- ☐ Fanny Pack
- ☐ Cosmetic Bag
- ☐ Shaving Kit
- ☐ Soap Dish with Soap
- ☐ Hand Sanitizer
- ☐ Travel Size Toiletries (i.e., Toothpaste, Shampoo & Conditioner, Shaving Cream, Cologne, etc.)
- ☐ Small Plastic Containers for Body Lotion, Moisturizer, etc.
- ☐ Toothbrush Cover
- ☐ Pill Containers
- ☐ Shower Cap
- ☐ Swimmer's Towel/Chamois
- ☐ Towelettes
- ☐ Small Tissue Packets
- ☐ Small Blow Dryer
- ☐ Mirror
- ☐ Suction Sink Stopper
- ☐ Utility Knife with Can Opener & Wine Opener
- ☐ Cutting Board
- ☐ Folding Cup
- ☐ Heating Cord
- ☐ Water Container
- ☐ Ice Pack
- ☐ Jewelry Case
- ☐ Camera & Film or Storage (i.e., Memory Cards, CDs)
- ☐ Camera Case/Equipment
- ☐ Film Shield

- ☐ Laundry Bag
- ☐ Spot Remover
- ☐ Laundry Soap (Regular & for Fine Fabrics)
- ☐ Clothes Hangers
- ☐ Clothes Pins
- ☐ Portable Clothesline
- ☐ Lint Pick-up
- ☐ Travel Iron or Steamer
- ☐ Small Sewing Kit
- ☐ Shoe Covers
- ☐ Travel Alarm Clock
- ☐ Folding Umbrella
- ☐ Lightweight Folding Raingear
- ☐ Maps
- ☐ Small Size Travel Games & Playing Cards
- ☐ Small First Aid Kit
- ☐ Ear Plugs
- ☐ Eyeshade

International Travel Items
- ☐ Passport
- ☐ Guide Books
- ☐ Foreign Language Dictionaries
- ☐ Money Belt
- ☐ Converter
- ☐ Adaptor Plugs
- ☐ Currency Converter
- ☐ Calculator
- ☐ Drinking Water Tablets or Solution

Chapter 26

Camping & Backpacking

This chapter is at least minimally inter-changeable with the previous chapter on **Travel**, but the focus here is on outdoor trips and their requisite supplies. Some of the items assume that you will be outdoors in inclement weather and may not apply if your outings will be in a location with a warm climate.

Camping & Backpacking

- ☐ Backpack
- ☐ Sleeping Bag
- ☐ Pillow & Pillow Case
- ☐ Cot
- ☐ Air Mattress & Pump or Foam Mat
- ☐ Groundcloth and/or Tarp
- ☐ Folding Chairs
- ☐ Tent & Stakes
- ☐ Lantern, Mantel, & Fuel

- ☐ Cookstove & Fuel
- ☐ Grill
- ☐ Charcoal
- ☐ Newspaper
- ☐ Matches (Waterproof) and/or Butane Lighter
- ☐ Ice Chest/Cooler
- ☐ Water & Water Containers
- ☐ Picnic Cloth

Cook Kit
- ☐ Stewing Pot(s) & Lid(s)
- ☐ Frying Pan

- [ ] Coffee Pot
- [ ] Unbreakable Plates & Bowls
- [ ] Unbreakable Cups
- [ ] Knives, Forks, & Spoons
- [ ] Serving and/or Grilling Utensils
- [ ] Sharp Knife
- [ ] Can Opener
- [ ] Cutting Board
- [ ] Thermos
- [ ] Dishpan
- [ ] Soap (i.e., Dish, Laundry, Bath Soap & Covered Soap Dish)
- [ ] Dishtowels
- [ ] Two-sided Sponge with Scouring Pad
- [ ] Tin Foil
- [ ] Food Wrap
- [ ] Food Storage Bags
- [ ] Trash Bags
- [ ] Paper Towels, Napkins, & Toilet Paper
- [ ] Rope (i.e., Nylon Utility Cord or 50 Foot Nylon Parachute Cord)
- [ ] Bungee Cords
- [ ] Clothespins
- [ ] Duct Tape
- [ ] Pocket Knife
- [ ] A Few Small Handtools (i.e., Ax, Small Broom or Rake, Shovel)
- [ ] Flyswatter

- [ ] Flashlight & Extra Batteries
- [ ] Portable Radio & Extra Batteries
- [ ] Canteen
- [ ] Compass
- [ ] Whistle
- [ ] Shower Sandals
- [ ] Sneakers
- [ ] Hiking Boots
- [ ] Wool Socks & Sock Liners
- [ ] Long Underwear
- [ ] Wool Hat
- [ ] Wool Gloves
- [ ] Brimmed Hat or Visor
- [ ] Bandana
- [ ] Waterproof Rainjacket
- [ ] Assorted Clothes to Layer, According to Weather
- [ ] Belt or Suspenders
- [ ] Dark Glasses (100% Ultraviolet Ray Blockage)
- [ ] Sunscreen
- [ ] Insect Repellant
- [ ] Lip Protector
- [ ] Vitamins and/or Prescription Medicine
- [ ] First Aid Kit, Including Band-Aids & Moleskin
- [ ] Needle & Thread
- [ ] Personal Items (i.e., Toothbrush, Toothpaste, Comb, etc.)
- [ ] Towels & Washcloths
- [ ] Beach Towel
- [ ] Beach Mat

Miscellaneous Items

☐ Cell Phone

☐ GPS

☐ Camera & Film or Storage (i.e., Memory Cards, CDs)

☐ Reading Material

☐ Cards & Games

☐ Notebook, Pen, & Pencil

☐ Envelopes & Stamps

☐ Maps

☐ Binoculars

☐ Small Musical Instrument

☐ Art Supplies

☐ Fishing Equipment

☐ Bicycle, Helmet, & Water Bottle

☐ Recreational Equipment (i.e., Frisbee, Balls, etc.)

Chapter 27

Books

(Fiction & Nonfiction)

The following list is fairly comprehensive in terms of the categories of books published. It is provided as a memory aid to help remind you of the kinds of books that are missing and those you will want to have when you begin to restock your bookshelves.

One way to figure your book losses for insurance purposes is to estimate the amount of shelf space you had for your books and to divide this shelf space by the average book size. Then multiply the approximate number of books by an estimated average book cost.

Books commonly found in many households include cookbooks, reference books (like a dictionary, a thesaurus, a set of encyclopedias, and a medical guide), work-related books, how-to books (such as guides to resume writing, household maintenance, gardening, and parenting), novels, "coffee table" books, and religious books.

Books (Fiction & Nonfiction)

☐ Adventure
☐ Agriculture/Horticulture
☐ Americana
☐ Animals
☐ Anthropology/Archaeology
☐ Autobiography

- ☐ Biography
- ☐ Business/Economics
- ☐ Catalogs
- ☐ Child Guidance/Parenting
- ☐ Communication
- ☐ Community/Public Affairs
- ☐ Computers/Electronics
- ☐ Consumer Affairs
- ☐ Cooking/Foods/Nutrition
- ☐ Counseling/Career Guidance
- ☐ Crafts
- ☐ Educational
- ☐ Entertainment/Games
- ☐ Ethnic
- ☐ Fantasy
- ☐ Fashion/Beauty
- ☐ Feminism
- ☐ Film/Cinema/Stage
- ☐ Gardening
- ☐ Gay/Lesbian
- ☐ General Nonfiction
- ☐ Geography
- ☐ Government/Politics
- ☐ Health/Medicine
- ☐ Historical Fiction
- ☐ History
- ☐ Hobby
- ☐ Horror
- ☐ How-to
- ☐ Humanities
- ☐ Humor
- ☐ Juvenile Books
- ☐ Labor/Management
- ☐ Language & Literature
- ☐ Law
- ☐ Literary Criticism
- ☐ Mainstream/Contemporary Fiction
- ☐ Marine Subjects
- ☐ Men's Issues & Subjects
- ☐ Military/War
- ☐ Money/Finance
- ☐ Music & Dance
- ☐ Mystery
- ☐ Novels
- ☐ Nature & Environment
- ☐ Philosophy
- ☐ Photography
- ☐ Picture Books
- ☐ Plays
- ☐ Poetry
- ☐ Psychology
- ☐ Real Estate
- ☐ Recreation
- ☐ Reference
- ☐ Regional
- ☐ Religion
- ☐ Romance
- ☐ Scholarly
- ☐ Science Fiction
- ☐ Science/Technology
- ☐ Self-help
- ☐ Short Story Collections
- ☐ Social Sciences
- ☐ Sociology
- ☐ Spiritual (New Age)

☐ Sports
☐ Technical
☐ Textbook
☐ Transportation
☐ Travel

☐ Western
☐ Women's Studies/Issues
☐ World Affairs
☐ Young Adult

Chapter 28

Music Categories

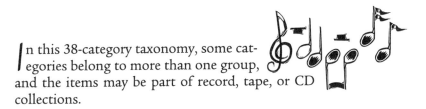

In this 38-category taxonomy, some categories belong to more than one group, and the items may be part of record, tape, or CD collections.

Music Categories

Country
- ☐ Bluegrass
- ☐ Contemporary
- ☐ Traditional Country

Jazz
- ☐ Bop (Bebop, Cool)
- ☐ Fusion (Bossa Nova, Jazz Soul, Smooth Jazz)
- ☐ Ragtime
- ☐ Swing

Modern Pop
- ☐ Adult Contemporary
- ☐ Dance (Dance Pop, Pop Rap, Techno)

- ☐ Smooth Jazz

Rap
- ☐ Hardcore Rap
- ☐ Pop Rap

Rhythm & Blues
- ☐ Blues (Blues Rock, Chicago Blues, Country Blues, Soul Blues)
- ☐ Funk
- ☐ Jazz Soul
- ☐ Rock & Roll
- ☐ Soul

Rock
- ☐ Classic Rock (Blues Rock, Hard Rock, Psychedelic)

☐ Modern Rock (Alternative Rock, Hard Rock, Metal, Punk)

Western Classical

☐ Baroque

☐ Classical

☐ Early Music (Medieval, Renaissance)

☐ Modern Classical

☐ Romantic

Western Folk

☐ Bluegrass

☐ Celtic

☐ Country Blues

☐ Flamenco

Worldbeat

☐ Latin (Bossa Nova, Salsa, Tango)

☐ Reggae

Miscellaneous Music

☐ Children's

☐ Big Band

☐ Gospel

☐ Opera

☐ Show Tunes

Chapter 29

Movie Genres

If you are a movie collector who has lost video cassettes or DVDs, the following list may remind you of what you are missing.

The Web site **www.createyourownscreenplay.com** can provide you with examples of fourteen basic movie genres to further jog your memory.

Main Genres

- ☐ Action (Disaster)
- ☐ Adventure
- ☐ Comedy
- ☐ Crime/Gangster
- ☐ Detective Story/Courtroom Drama
- ☐ Drama (Coming-of Age, Historical, Social)
- ☐ Epic/Myth
- ☐ Horror
- ☐ Love/Romance
- ☐ Musicals
- ☐ Science Fiction
- ☐ Westerns

Some Sub-Genres

- ☐ Art Film
- ☐ Black Comedy
- ☐ Buddy Movie
- ☐ Biographicals
- ☐ Detective/Mystery
- ☐ Disaster
- ☐ Fantasy
- ☐ Film Noir
- ☐ Ghost Story
- ☐ The Heist (or Caper)
- ☐ Picaresque
- ☐ Sports
- ☐ Thriller/Suspense

Chapter 30

Art, Hobbies, & Collections

The arts generally refer to art, literature, music, and drama. This section does not do justice to professionals in these areas, nor will it be of much help to collectors of fine art. It may be useful, however, for those who enjoy certain artistic activities during their leisure time.

One definition of the word hobby is something that a person likes to do or study in his or her spare time—a favorite pastime or avocation. Because there are almost endless possibilities here, this chapter cannot be considered complete. The following lists attempt to mention some of the most common things that people do, study, or collect.

Hobbies

- ☐ Photography
- ☐ Painting, Sketching & Drawing
- ☐ Calligraphy
- ☐ Crafts
- ☐ Scrapbooking
- ☐ Sewing
- ☐ Handcrafts (i.e., Knitting, Crocheting, Embroidery, Needlepoint, Weaving, Quilting, Macramé)
- ☐ Jewelry Making
- ☐ Flower Arranging
- ☐ Sculpting
- ☐ Pottery/Ceramics
- ☐ Stained Glass Making
- ☐ Music (Playing Musical Instruments)
- ☐ Home Decorating

☐ Furniture Refinishing
☐ Woodworking/Carpentry
☐ Home Improvements
☐ Car Repair
☐ Electronics
☐ Model Trains
☐ Model Building
☐ Gardening
☐ Bird Watching
☐ Astronomy/Stargazing
☐ Science Experimenting
☐ Collecting Things

Hobby Aids

Some tools are mentioned here briefly. For more complete lists see "Tools" in the **Storage** *section and also in "Outdoor Garden & Maintenance" in the* **Outdoor Living and Maintenance** *section. More sewing supplies are given in* **Storage** *under "Sewing Kit."*

☐ Camera Equipment, Film &/or Memory Storage, Darkroom Equipment
☐ Digital Software & Hardware
☐ Video Camera/Camcorder
☐ Movie Camera, Projector & Screen
☐ Slide/video Projector

Art & Crafts Supplies
☐ Canvas
☐ Easel
☐ Tote Board
☐ Portfolio
☐ Carrying Cases

☐ Portable Chair & Umbrella
☐ Sketching Pad
☐ Pallet
☐ Pallet Knives
☐ Ruler
☐ Scissors
☐ Special Paper (i.e., Watercolor, Poster Board, Colored, Construction, Transfer, Calligraphy, Art Tissue, Card Stock)
☐ Color Wheel
☐ Pencils, Assorted, including Water Color
☐ Erasers
☐ Calligraphy Lettering Set
☐ Collage Supplies
☐ Cellophane Envelopes for Prints & Cards
☐ Paints (i.e., Watercolors, Oils, Liquid Tempura, Stencil)
☐ Paint Crayons
☐ Marking Pens
☐ Charcoals
☐ Pastels
☐ Oil Pastels
☐ Paint Brushes
☐ Sponges
☐ Miskits
☐ Paint Thinner
☐ Median
☐ X-Acto Knife
☐ Mat Cutter
☐ Precut Mats

☐ Frames & Frame Kits

☐ Stapling Tacker & Staples

☐ T Square

☐ Triangular Square

☐ Stencils

☐ Sewing Machine & Supplies (i.e., Dress Form, Patterns)

☐ Sewing Kit (See list of sewing supplies in **Storage Spaces** Section)

☐ Handwork Patterns

☐ Knitting Needles & Yarn

☐ Crochet Kit

☐ Embroidery Kit

☐ Needlepoint Kit

☐ Weaving Equipment (i.e., Loom or Spinning Wheel) & Supplies

☐ Quilting Kit

☐ Macramé Kit

☐ Art Needlework Mounting Board & Tape

☐ Scrapbooking Supplies (i.e., Adhesives, Albums, Books, Die Cuts/Cut Outs, Embellishments, Embossing, Ink/Chalk/ Rub-Ons, Layout Kits, Papers, Pens & Pencils, Printers, Scanners, Software, Stamping, Stickers, storage, Templates, Tools)

☐ Miscellaneous Craft Supplies (i.e., Craft Sticks, Beads, Wires & Sequins; Glue & Stains; Modeling Clay & Spatulas; Ribbons & Lace & Velcro; Decals & Rubber Art Stamps; T-Shirt Art Supplies; Marbelizing Kit; Glue Gun)

☐ Jewelry Making Supplies

Floral Supplies

☐ Dried & Artificial Flowers

☐ Baskets, Vases, Pots, Wreaths, etc.

☐ Planter Moss or Lichen

☐ Accessories (i.e., Wire, Tape, Picks, Clay)

☐ Pottery Kit

Music-related Items

☐ Musical Instruments

☐ Music Stand

☐ Sheet Music

☐ Instrument Cases and/or Covers

☐ Supplies for Cleaning & Repairing Instruments

☐ Shop Tools (i.e., for Metal, Woodworking, Stone, Ceramics, Stained Glass, etc.)

☐ Carpenter's Apron

☐ Lapidary Supplies (i.e., Rock Polisher, Tumbler)

☐ Mechanical Tools (i.e., for Car Repair, etc.)

- ☐ Hobby Electronics Supplies & Tools (i.e., Wire, Batteries, Small Motors, Volt Meter, Soldering Gun)
- ☐ Model Railroad Supplies
- ☐ Model Building Kits & Supplies (i.e., Glue, Paint, Brushes)
- ☐ Gardening Tools
- ☐ Binoculars
- ☐ Telescope
- ☐ Tripod
- ☐ Magnifying Glass
- ☐ Science Kits (i.e., Chemistry Set)
- ☐ Insect Net
- ☐ Miscellaneous Hobby Supplies & Equipment (i.e., Metal Detector)
- ☐ Special Interest & Instruction Books
- ☐ Display Materials for Hobbies & Collections (i.e., Display Cases, Lighting)

Collections

- ☐ Antiques
- ☐ Fine Art
- ☐ Coins
- ☐ Wine
- ☐ Dolls
- ☐ Stuffed Animals
- ☐ Guns
- ☐ Rare Books
- ☐ Model Trains
- ☐ Masks
- ☐ Rocks/Stones
- ☐ Sea Shells
- ☐ Trophies & Medals
- ☐ Stamps
- ☐ Miniatures
- ☐ Memorabilia (i.e., Theater, Sports, Military)
- ☐ Commemorative Pins & Buttons
- ☐ Posters
- ☐ Baseball and/or Other Trading Cards
- ☐ Comic Books
- ☐ Matchbooks
- ☐ Miscellaneous Collectibles

Chapter 31

The Car

ar is not meant to be an exclu-sive term here and includes other modes of transportation, such as SUVs, trucks, and vans. Some of the items listed are things most of us carry inside our vehicles or in their storage spaces (i.e., maps and insurance information). A number of the other items mentioned are included in case of an emergency. Additional items that are not necessarily carried inside cars but are nevertheless associated with them and/or their care and maintenance are listed here also.

The Car

In the Car or Trunk

- ☐ Car Insurance Information
- ☐ Car Registration
- ☐ Owner's Manual
- ☐ Emergency Road Service Handbook
- ☐ Auto Association Information & ID Card

- ☐ Cell Phone Accessories
- ☐ Maps
- ☐ Windshield Scraper/Squeegee
- ☐ Spray Bottle of Water
- ☐ A Rag or Two
- ☐ Deodorizer
- ☐ Infant/Child Car Seat
- ☐ Tire Chains or Cables Tire Chains or Cables

☐ Jumper Cables
☐ Road Flares
☐ Flashlight & Extra Batteries
☐ Portable Radio & Extra Batteries
☐ Ground Cloth
☐ Work Gloves
☐ A Tool Kit (i.e., Screwdrivers, Pliers, Crescent Wrench)
☐ Sand/Rock Salt
☐ Disposable Camera
☐ First Aid Kit
☐ Water
☐ Food Bars
☐ Whistle
☐ Paper, Pen, or Pencil
☐ Dust Masks

☐ Blanket
☐ Sturdy Shoes
☐ Warm Jacket

Also for the Car/Vehicle

☐ Luggage Rack
☐ Ski Rack
☐ Bike Rack
☐ Quart of Oil
☐ Coolant
☐ Transmission Fluid
☐ Power Steering Fluid
☐ Tire Pressure Gauge
☐ Whisk Broom
☐ Bucket
☐ Chamois
☐ Car Shampoo
☐ Towels
☐ Car Wax

Chapter 32

Records, Documents, & The Safe Deposit Box

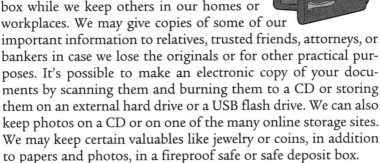

All of us have important papers and records that require safekeeping. We may store some of these in a safe deposit box while we keep others in our homes or workplaces. We may give copies of some of our important information to relatives, trusted friends, attorneys, or bankers in case we lose the originals or for other practical purposes. It's possible to make an electronic copy of your documents by scanning them and burning them to a CD or storing them on an external hard drive or a USB flash drive. We can also keep photos on a CD or on one of the many online storage sites. We may keep certain valuables like jewelry or coins, in addition to papers and photos, in a fireproof safe or safe deposit box.

Following are the kinds of records, documents, and personal items that are important to find, recall, or recount after a disaster.

Items for Safe Keeping

- ☐ Will (Plus Codicils, if applicable)
- ☐ List of Special Bequests
- ☐ Titles & Deeds, Including Mortgages
- ☐ Lease Agreements
- ☐ Notes & Loan Agreements
- ☐ Lines of Credit
- ☐ Birth Certificate
- ☐ Marriage License
- ☐ Citizenship Papers

Insurance Policies

- ☐ Health
- ☐ Auto
- ☐ Property (Homeowners or Renters)
- ☐ Life
- ☐ Long Term Care
- ☐ Disability
- ☐ Business
- ☐ Title
- ☐ Other (i.e., Professional Liability)

☐ Powers of Attorney

☐ Trust Agreements & Documents

☐ Employment Contracts

☐ Partnership Agreements

☐ Business Agreements/Contracts

☐ Auto/Vehicle Ownership Certificate

☐ Boat Records

☐ House Plans/Blueprints

☐ Financial Plan

Investment Records

- ☐ Brokerage Account Records
- ☐ Stock Certificates
- ☐ Mutual Fund Records
- ☐ Certificates of Deposit
- ☐ Bonds
- ☐ Limited Partnerships
- ☐ Other Securities
- ☐ Deferred Compensation
- ☐ IRA or Keough Plans
- ☐ Annuity Contracts
- ☐ Stock-option Plan
- ☐ Stock-purchase Plan
- ☐ Profit-sharing Plan
- ☐ Income & Gift Tax Returns

☐ Tax Returns

☐ Bank Statements & Cancelled Checks

☐ Retirement Papers

☐ Pension Plans

☐ Military Discharge Papers

Public Benefits Records

- ☐ Social Security
- ☐ Worker's Compensation Benefits
- ☐ Public Medical Insurance
- ☐ Job Training Program Services

Court Decrees

- ☐ Divorce/Separation Records
- ☐ Adoption Papers
- ☐ Custody and/or Guardianship Papers
- ☐ Lawsuit Settlements

☐ Passport

Record of Important Numbers (Plus their Addresses, Phone Numbers & Cancellation Instructions, if Applicable)

- ☐ Social Security
- ☐ Driver's License
- ☐ Checking Accounts
- ☐ Savings Accounts
- ☐ Credit Cards

☐ Safe Combination

Medical Records & Health History

☐ Major Illnesses, Accidents & Medical conditions

☐ Prescriptions

☐ Known Allergies

☐ Summary of Immunizations

☐ Hospitalizations, Including Surgeries

☐ Family Health Histories

☐ Physicians & Medical Centers Used

☐ Health Care Directive to Physicians

☐ Durable Power of Attorney for Health Care

Keepsake Documents

☐ Diplomas

☐ Awards, Certificates of Merit, Honors

☐ Religious Certificates (i.e., Baptismal, Bar Mitzvah, etc.)

☐ Professional Licensure, Certification, etc.

☐ Student Transcripts

☐ Records of Family Histories/Genealogies

☐ Journals

☐ Manuscripts

☐ Correspondence

☐ Computer Diskettes & CDs

☐ Purchase Agreements & Records, including Warranties

☐ Credit History

☐ Before-need Funeral Instructions

☐ Cemetery Plot Deeds

☐ List of Stored or Loaned Items

☐ List of Debts or Money Owed to you

List of Contacts with Names & Addresses

☐ Relatives & Friends

☐ Professional, Fraternal & Other Organizations & Memberships

☐ Business Contacts, Associates, Prospects

List of Safe or Safe Deposit Items in Addition to Papers

☐ Jewelry

☐ Coins or Coin Collections

☐ Cash

☐ Photo Negatives and/or Digital "Flash Cards"

Personal Property Inventory

☐ General Written Inventory

☐ Appraisals

☐ List of Valuables (i.e., Antiques, Family Heirlooms, Jewelry)

☐ Photo Record (Snapshots, Memory Cards and/or Video) of Household Inventory & Other Personal Property

Chapter 33

Shopping Green

Shopping "green" reflects growing concern about the environment. Surveys suggest that most of us want to do our part to make the world a better place. We are recycling more, and we are becoming more selective about what we buy as we become more aware of the connection between what we consume and the environment.

If you are rebuilding and/or restocking a home, you are in an ideal position to consider purchasing sustainably produced products—products that are produced from renewable resources rather than ones that deplete the earth's nonrenewable resources. This will have a positive effect on the environment. By shopping green you can help to conserve energy, reduce garbage, and reduce air and water pollution.

The first thing we can do as individuals is to precycle. Precycling means making environmentally sound decisions while we shop by paying attention to packaging (avoiding plastic goods, overpackaged items, and items that can't be reused, refilled, or recycled), by not buying disposable items (like razors, diapers, and Styrofoam cups), and by buying in bulk. Taking reusable bags on shopping trips saves paper and plastic. Where you shop may also be important.

Resources are available to guide environmentally conscious shoppers. A good place to start is Co-op America, an organization whose mission is "to harness economic power—the strength of consumers, investors, businesses, and the marketplace—to create a socially just and environmentally sustainable society." It publishes an annual edition of *National Green Pages*, which is "the only nationwide directory of screened, socially and environmentally responsible businesses coast to coast." This 200+ page directory lists practical products and services from cleaning products to furniture to gardening supplies, and includes green consumer tips, fair trade and sweatshop-free information and products.

Co-op America
1612 K Street NW, suite 600
Washington, DC 200006
800-584-7336
www.coopamerica.org

Shopping for a Better World: The Quick and Easy Guide to All Your Socially Responsible Shopping by Benjamin Hollister, Rosalyn Will, and Alice Tapper Marlin, published by Sierra Club Books, is "a quick and easy guide to all socially responsible shopping." It contains information about more than 200 companies, more than 2,100 popular brand names, and 23 consumer product categories. Each of the well-known companies has been graded by the Council on Economic Priorities (CEP) on its environmental performance and 6 social issue areas.

The Consumer's Guide to Effective Environmental Choices: Practical Advice from the Union of Concerned Scientists by Michael Brower and Warren Leon endorses steps to take to live more ecologically based lifestyles as consumers of the earth's resources, including "Seven Rules for Responsible Consumption." In addition to providing sound, practical advice, based on thoughtful analysis of the way ordinary daily actions affect the environment, it also contains a resource list of active Web sites, books, and periodicals for additional information.

Green Living: The E Magazine Handbook for Living Lightly on the Earth by E Magazine, a Plume 320-page paperback, has many practical tips on a green lifestyle, including chapters on cleaning your home without chemicals and buying natural-fiber clothes and pesticide-free baby food. The online home of "E/Environmental Magazine," *www.emagazine.com*, has an extensive online directory of environmental products and services. It offers a mix of features, news, and lifestyle stories and covers all the emerging issues, along with contact information. Subscriptions are offered for both online and paper editions.

Chapter 34

Preparing for Emergencies: Learning from Experience

A number of years ago I attended a workshop during which participants were given an exercise that seems worth repeating here. We were asked to sit down for ten minutes, paper and pen in hand, and make a list of what we would take from our homes if we had to evacuate in a hurry.

The point of the exercise was to help us take a look at our values. What we decided to take from our homes reflected what we considered to be most important to us. Days, even weeks, later I was still coming up with things that I'd forgotten to write down during the short exercise.

Ten minutes isn't much time to think about our most prized possessions and those things that become important to us if we no longer have them. During an actual emergency, most people don't have the luxury of thinking clearly. Instead, they are asked to act, and to act fast. So preparedness requires, among other things, making and maintaining inventories of your household goods and noting those items that you would want to take with you in case of an emergency.

Create a Personal Property Inventory

Anyone who has survived a loss of home by disaster knows the importance of keeping accurate inventories for insurance and tax purposes and also to help replace what was lost. It is essential, for instance, to have a written inventory of what's in your household, along with descriptions and prices when appropriate. A copy of your inventory should be kept in a safe deposit box or in some location other than your home. You may want to include other important documents in this location away from your home in case of an area-wide disaster. Your insurance company may want to have a copy of your inventory, and, of course, part of your advance planning should include making sure that you have adequate insurance coverage.

In addition to having a written record, having a pictorial inventory is also important. Take snapshots of anything of value, such as fine art, antiques, furniture, jewelry, and so on. Note identification marks such as numbers, letters, or signatures on valuable items like Wedgwood, cut glass, figurines, and so on. These markings should also be noted on any appraisals or certificates of value that you have. With a digital camera, it's now possible to keep photos on CDs. Again, one set of prints or CDs should be kept off the premises in a secure location.

A video record is a specialized type of inventory that can easily capture the important details of your home (noting special architectural features or custom work), as well as the contents, as it pans each room. You can do this yourself, or you can hire a professional to do it for you. Some people like to include verbal descriptions or interesting anecdotes about significant items to pass along to future generations. A video recording or your home is especially important for architects and designers whose job it is to rebuild a home lost to a disaster. Insurance companies can use videos to see the physical details that may be difficult to remember and to recapture. Because videos tend to degrade over time, you may want to transfer your recording to a DVD.

It's wise to keep a copy of your video or DVD in a safe deposit box or to give it to a close relative or friend, but not to a person who lives in your immediate neighborhood. The yellow pages list these services under *Video Production Services* and under *Photographers* in other directories.

Advance Planning for Evacuation

Take time to make a list of the items you would want to take in case you had to evacuate on short notice. The list might include expensive items like jewelry, antiques, and fine art, but it might also include treasures that have sentimental value such as old letters, genealogies, or a child's first painting. You should consider items of a practical nature like insurance and tax information, property records, and other important papers listed in **Records, Documents, & The Safe Deposit Box** along with your emergency supplies. It's a good idea to include everyday practical things like a calendar/planner, address book, prescription drugs, clothes for 1 to 3 days, eyeglasses or contact lenses, money, credit cards, and identification.

Be sure you take contact information for friends and family who live out of the area. You can keep a list of the most important addresses and phone numbers in your wallet so you will have them with you even if you don't have time to grab your address book. If you have a cell phone, remember to take it and your charger.

After you make your basic evacuation list, set your priorities. Decide what you would grab first, next, and so on, keeping various time frames in mind. Note the location of each item on your list, and be specific. For instance, photograph albums, family records, and personal writings are at the top of most people's lists. Keep in mind that some albums or framed pictures may be in plain sight and easy to get to, whereas other photographs are in a stack of boxes in a closet. One fire survivor suggests putting doubled and neatly folded garbage bags somewhere near photograph albums and other collections in order to have something in which to put them on short notice.

Be sure to share ideas so that everyone in your home has a say in what's important and that everyone knows where to find the items you want to take when you evacuate. You might even have a practice drill, assigning each person a role to play. Be sure to keep your evacuation list handy enough for family members to access it easily but not in a place conspicuous enough for an outsider to stumble across it.

Think about how you would gather your priority items in a hurry in an actual emergency, assuming you have some time available to you. One tip from former disaster survivors is to think like a burglar. For example, have garbage bags handy and use the layers of your bedding (excluding a cumbersome bedspread or comforter) to bundle things up and haul them away quickly. As part of your advance planning it also makes sense to note the location of luggage, boxes, and empty shopping bags for collecting and transporting your things.

There are certainly occasions when an emergency is so pressing that it is not possible to retrieve any items from your home. However, according to one emergency service coordinator, most evacuations allow at least 30 minutes for residents to leave home from the time an evacuation order is issued. The average evacuation time for a slow-moving event is more than an hour. These events include some area-wide fires, floods, or slow-moving hazardous material incidents. A best-case scenario allows up to 6 hours or more. When this is the case, it's a good idea to have a contact list and a list of emergency resources, including whom to call, such as a moving and storage company or people you know with a truck. It's possible for a 1,700 square foot house to be pretty well cleared out in less than 6 hours if you have a plan and adequate resources. In the case of floods, it may be possible to take time to raise some items off the floor or to move them to a higher level, like a second story or attic.

Emergency Preparedness Planning

Every household should have an emergency preparedness plan for two contingencies—the first for evacuating your home and the second for staying put. When you plan for evacuation, it's important to identify escape routes and to assign meeting places. FEMA and the Red Cross suggest designating two gathering spots—one location a safe distance from your home and another place outside your neighborhood in case you can't return home.

If you have to evacuate, you should lock your home, and, *only if instructed*, turn off the water, gas, and electricity. Put messages on your door and answering machine, saying where you can be found and who is with you. Include the date and time of the message, and notify out-of-area contacts.as soon as possible.

Some disasters require people to "shelter in place" or to stay home. Hazardous materials incidents and earthquakes in particular come to mind, but they are not the only ones. Especially after the devastating hurricanes of 2005, local state, and national emergency services organizations request that every household be self-sufficient for at least 72 hours—whether you are asked to evacuate or to stay where you are. This means having a well-maintained stock of emergency supplies, including plenty of food, water, and medical supplies. Look in the **Emergency Supplies** chapter for more details. The Red Cross and many local agencies not only have recommendations about supplies but also offer resources and specific information about emergency preparedness for your geographical area.

Index

abatements, 48
actual cash value (ACV; fair market value; FMV),
    25, 37
  appraisals of, 59
  negotiation of, 41
  receipts and, 54
  vs. replacement cost, 12, 24, 37–38
additional living expenses (ALE), 20, 21, 53, 68–69
adjusters
  abatements and, 48
  depreciation and, 37
  keeping notes for, 20–21
  misinformation from, 16, 50
  for personal property claims, 12
  public, 32, 42, 47
  quick settlements with, 29–30, 47–48
  scope of loss preparation, 47
  second opinions and, 22, 44–45, 52
air quality testing, 48
ALE (additional living expenses), 21
appraisal process, 54–55
assertiveness, 21, 28
assistance payment status, 69
attorneys
  for insurance company, 32
  for policyholders, 31–32, 50–51

building code or ordinance coverage, 18, 24

casualty loss, 56-57, 64-66
causation, 49
CDs, for personal property inventory creation, 160
cell phones, 3-4
change of address notifications, 6-7
charitable donations, 5-6
children, coping with loss, 7-8
claimants, 28
contents coverage (coverage C), 18, 35-36
contents inventory, 38, 40, 54
contents loss, 20
Contents/Personal Property Coverage (Coverage C),
    18, 35-36
contingent fees, 32-33
contract law, principles of, 22-23
contractors, 44-46
    mediation of estimates, 54-55
    scope of loss preparation, 47
contra proferenum, 23
Co-op America, 157
coping, helping children with, 7-8
cost assignments, for personal property inventory,
    11-12
coverage A. See dwelling coverage
coverage C (contents coverage), 18, 35-36
credit card, for tracking disaster-related expenses, 63
credit card companies, identifying replacement costs
    and, 41

declarations page, of insurance policy, 17
demolition, government-ordered, 64
denial, grief and, 13
depreciation, 38
    negotiation of, 41-42
    subjectivity of, 41-42, 53-54
disaster assistance centers, 4
documentation
    of amount/type of repairs, 43-44
    of destroyed/damaged property, 40-41
    for insurance company, 16, 38
    of major loss, 48
    of pre-loss property, 43

donations, 5–6
DVDs, for personal property inventory creation, 160
dwelling coverage (coverage A), 18
    claims, negotiating settlement of, 44
    limits of, 36
dwelling loss, 19–20

emergency preparedness plan, 162–163
endorsement codes, 36
environmental hygienist, 48
"Equivalent Construction" Limited Dwelling
        Coverage, 26–27
ERC (extended replacement coverage), 18, 24, 25
EUO (examination under oath), 29
evacuation, advanced planning for, 161–162
examination under oath (EUO), 29
exclusions, 25–26
extended replacement coverage (ERC), 18, 24, 25

fair claims settlements, 50
fair market value (FMV). See actual cash value
FEMA (Federal Emergency Management Agency),
        4, 57, 162
financial assistance, sources of, 4
FMV (fair market value). See actual cash value
Form 536, 64
Form 4684, 59, 64

gift registry scanners, 40
GRC (guaranteed replacement coverage), 24, 25
"green shopping," 156–158
grief, stages of, 13–14
guaranteed replacement coverage (GRC), 24, 25

help, getting, 16–17
home
    inspection, 48
    services, disconnecting, 4–5
    temporary loss of use. See additional living
        expenses (ALE)
homeowner's insurance policy, 3
household inventory. See personal property inventory
housing, temporary, 3

indemnity, 23
information sharing, among disaster victims, 27–28
insurance adjusters. See adjusters
insurance agent, notifying, 19
insurance claim disputes
    legal aspects of, 23
    policyholder rights and, 28–29, 32
    scope of loss differences and, 47
insurance claims
    collection of benefits, 30
    complaints about, 30–31
    depreciation and, 53–54
    filing, 19
    final or full, 29–30
    for large-scale disaster survivors, 39–40
    mistakes on forms, 29
    padding, 28, 43
    payment of, 16
    personal property, 13–14
    professional help with, 31–33
    rejection of, 50
    reporting, 16, 17
    submitting contents part of, 37
insurance companies
    communication with, 20
    contents inventory list, 38
    cooperating with, 28–29
    duties of, 22
    government oversight of, 17
    notifying, 19
    personal property claims adjusters, 12
    pricing guidelines for, 52
    as profit-making businesses, 16, 50
    quick settlements with, 47–48
    recorded statements for, 29
    reputation of, 52
    scope of loss and, 47
    state regulation of, 30–31
    waiver of inventory requirements, 39
insurance coverage
    exclusions, 22–24, 49
    independent opinions for, 22
    "like kind and quality," 26, 60–61

for repairing/replacing contents, 36
insurance policy, 3
    declarations page of, 17
    duties of insurance company, 22
    endorsements, 17, 18
    exclusions, 25–26
    legal aspects of, 22–23
    limits of coverage, 18–19
    rights of insurer, 22, 28
insurance proceeds, gain from, 65–68
Internal Revenue Service. See IRS
Internet
    cost assignments for personal property
        inventory, 11–12
    shopping/pricing information, 40
IRS
    amended returns, 57–58
    deductibility guidelines for casualty loss, 57
    disaster-related tax relief, 57–60
    Form 4684, 59–60, 62
    Form 1040X, 59, 61–62
    like-kind replacement, 60–61
    on-line resources, 70
    publications, 59, 65, 67
    recordkeeping for disaster victims, 63–64
    refund for disaster loss, 56–57
    renters, tax relief for, 61
    replacement home tax tips, 66–68
    sample tax worksheet, 61–63
    taxable gain, 64–68
    tax forms, for disaster-related tax relief, 59–60
    tax questions, answering, 71
    tax relief assistance payments, 69
    temporary living expenses and, 68–69

Katrina disaster, 57, 67–68, 70

large-scale natural disasters, normal claims rules
        and, 39
law
    contract, principles of, 22–23
    relating to insurance claims, 49
lawsuits, 50–51

"like kind and quality" exclusions, 26, 60–61
limited testing, 45
"line of sight," 27
lists, 73–74
    content inventory, 35
    from insurance companies, 11
    personal property, 5
    for personal property inventory, 10, 11
Louisiana property taxes, 71–72

mediation, for contractor estimates, 54–55
mold/mildew, 48

National Flood Insurance Program (NFIP), 52
National Green Pages, 157
negotiation, 39–42
    of actual cash values, 41
    of depreciated items, 41
    of dwelling claims settlement, 44
    of fair claims settlement, 16, 50–51
neighbors
    help with personal property inventory, 10–11
    sharing information among, 27–28
net operating losses (NOLs), 64
networking, 8
New York Liberty Zone, 68
NFIP (National Flood Insurance Program), 52
NOLs (net operating losses), 64

obligations, for contents inventory claims, 38
organization
    for insurance claim settlement, 16, 19
    for recovery process, 5–8
overhead & profit (O&P), 53

partial damage," uniform and consistent repairs" for,
    44–45, 54
payment, for professional claim help, 32
percentage fee agreements, 33
personal property claim, 13–14
personal property inventory
    completing, 8–9
    cost assignments for, 11–12

creating, 160
final report, 12-13
forgotten "stuff," 10
friends/neighbors and, 10-11
revisiting rooms for, 9-10
personal property lists, 5
photographs, for personal property, 64, 160
policyholder (insured), 32
precycling, 156
prescriptions, 2
presidentially declared disaster, gain on insurance
     proceeds from, 65-66, 67
pricing guidelines, for labor and materials, 52
property, returning to "uniform and consistent
     appearance," 27, 44-45
property policies, types of, 25
property taxes, 71-72
public adjusters
     fair settlement claims and, 32
     hiring, 42
     scope of loss preparation, 47

real estate taxes, 71
rebuilding/repair estimates, independent, 45
receipts
     actual cash value and, 54
     for temporary/additional living expenses, 20
recorded statements, for insurance company, 29
recordkeeping, for disaster victims, 63-64
Recovery & Claim Diary, 20, 28, 34
recovery process, 1-2
     help during, 15-16
     organizing for, 5-8
release forms, 30
relocation
     determining replacement/repair costs of original
          home for, 45
     government-ordered, 64
renters
     insurance for, 3
     tax relief for, 61

repairs/replacement
    taxable gain and, 64–65
    "uniform and consistent," 27, 44–45, 54
replacement cost (RC), 11–12, 24, 37–38
replacement coverage, 25
replacement home, tax tips, 66–68

"scheduled" personal property items, 18
schools, 7–8
"scope of loss," 44, 46–47
second opinions, 22, 44–45, 52
state insurance commissioners (regulators), 30–31

taxable gain, 64–68
tax refund, for disaster loss, 56–57
tax relief, disaster-related. See IRS
tax relief assistance payments, 69
temporary living expenses. See additional living
    expenses

underinsurance, 23–24
"uniform and consistent" appearance, 27, 44–45, 54
United Policyholders (UP), 17, 19, 33
utilities and services, 4-5, 162

videos, for personal property inventory creation, 160

waiver forms, 30

Notes

Notes

Notes